52 Scrapbooking challenges

by Elsie Flannigan

- A year's worth of fun scrapbooking challenges
- Discover your personal style
- Release your scrapbooking creativity

contents

52 Scrapbooking Challenges

foreword

You know how you walk outside after a long, cold winter and feel the first warmth of the spring sun on your face? I always pause for a moment and savor the glow. Know that feeling I'm talking about? That's exactly the feeling I get when I look at the work of Elsie Flannigan. Warm. Free. Wide-open. And oh-so-welcome! Attention given to hand-wrought art and hand-written words. Her not-too-careful style is, in a word, pure. Pure art, pure passion, pure scrapbooking.

Know another feeling I get when I look at Elsie's work? (Shhhh…don't tell Elsie). I don't think she knows there are rules in scrapbooking. Here's what I mean: take a look at her layout titled "Soothing" on page 133. Boy, are the scrapbook police going to get her for that one—I see at least three broken rules. Know what? It's one of my favorite layouts I've ever seen. I love every little thing about it. Know why? Because she broke all the rules!

So, my hat's off to Elsie Flannigan. Her "don't fence me in" approach to her scrap-booking is sunshine to my soul—her open and heartfelt words, her everything-by-hand artwork. You law-abiding scrapbookers out there could take a lesson or two from Elsie. Go ahead—have some fun.

Elsie, you're amazing. My only advice for you is to keep doing exactly what you're doing. Bringing passion, art, words with heart, and freedom to scrapbooking. Everything about you is feisty and fun—my kind of girl.

intro

Life is a journey. It's inspiring and challenging and beautiful. In fact, you'll find beauty in every day if you look for it. I've found that the more I open my eyes—the more I search and observe and reflect on beauty—the more I see. And the more I'm inspired. Inspiration can come in the most unexpected places. I might find a pattern I like in some old wallpaper or a font I love on a restaurant sign, or I'll sketch a few photo ideas while I'm watching a movie with my husband. There is nothing more inspiring than everyday life!

Once I'm inspired, it's time to translate that inspiration onto a scrapbook page—a challenge I love to take. I work best when I'm challenged. I sometimes dare myself to find a new use for an old product or to find a way to incorporate a clothing style I love onto a layout. This gets my creativity flowing and my brain searching for new possibilities. I think it's important to enjoy the whole process of creating, from collecting ideas to putting the finishing touches on a layout. The more I take time to enjoy the process, the more rewarding and fulfilling this hobby is!

I want to share inspiration with you! I want to challenge you to stretch yourself creatively. I want to help you develop your personal style and tap into your true voice. I hope you enjoy these challenges and activities. I hope you discover many new things about yourself and your instincts. And remember: enjoy the journey!

Elsie

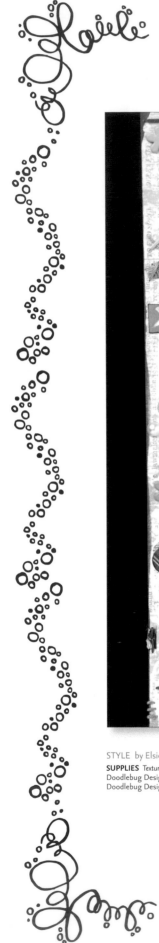

Every couple has a style, an essence, things that make them unique... We are casual, eclectic, we love vintage stuff, local Art, pug puppies, old music, ethnic foods, emotional color mixes, and plenty of time hanging out together!

STYLE by Elsie Flannigan

SUPPLIES Textured cardstock: Bazzill Basics Paper; Patterned papers: K&Company and KI Memories; Title: KI Memories; Ribbon: Doodlebug Design, American Crafts and C.M. Offray & Son; Adhesive pearls: Making Memories; Brads: Making Memories and Doodlebug Design; Epoxy accents and pillow button: MOD, Autumn Leaves; Other: Coin, thread, rhinestones and key ring.

The Challenges

challenge #1

Work Those Words

Whether it's a quote, a list of your favorite adjectives or computer-generated phrases, journaling on strips of cardstock is a great way to add visual excitement to your page. Be creative and cut a favorite quote into pieces to add to your design.

Love

is

friendship

set

on

fire.

~Jeremy

Taylor

MY MAN IS (on opposite page) by Elsie Flannigan
SUPPLIES Textured cardstock: Chatterbox; Patterned papers: Making Memories and Christina Cole for Provo Craft; Acrylic paint: Heidi Swapp for Advantus; Sticker and brad: American Crafts; Rub-ons: Making Memories; Pen: Sakura; Other: Corduroy and rhinestones.

LOVE IS by Elsie Flannigan
SUPPLIES Textured cardstock: Bazzill Basics Paper; Patterned paper: Scenic Route Paper Co.; Ribbon: American Crafts and C.M. Offray & Son; Photo corner: Heidi Swapp for Advantus; Pen: Uni-ball, Sanford; Flowers: Prima; Other: Buttons and thread.

MY SISTER by Mellette Berezoski
SUPPLIES Patterned papers: BasicGrey; Textured cardstock: FiberMark; Fabric swatches and vintage buttons: Making Memories; Muslin fabric paper: me & my BIG ideas; Index tabs: 7gypsies; Post-it, 3M; Rhinestone brads: Magic Scraps and SEI; Photo anchor and decorative rub-on: 7gypsies; Ribbon: Strano Designs; Label tape: Dymo; Computer font: High Strung, downloaded from www.dafont.com.

fun-loving

goofy

scary movie fanatic

collector of board games

youngest child

People magazine junkie

lover of cross word puzzles

avid sock wearer

camping enthusiast

master of the karaoke

warm, spirited, one of a kind

love her

MY

SISTER

challenge #2

Focus on One Photo

Convert a favorite photograph into a black-and-white image, then use it as the focal-point photo on your page. It will draw your viewer's eye right into the essence of your layout!

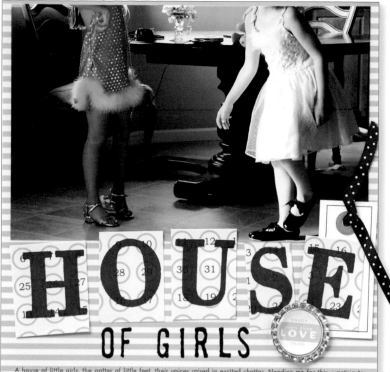

HOUSE
OF GIRLS

A house of little girls, the patter of little feet, their voices raised in excited chatter. Needing me for this, wanting to show me that. A part of my life right now. Girls and their friends, playing exuberantly, creating their own little world of fun and dreams and make believe. Finding their styles, learning their likes and dislikes, teaching each other, learning so much from each other. Just like a play in my own house, they are entertaining, delightful. I love being mom to girls. Love meeting their friends, seeing them interact, watching their personalities develop. Love capturing the little pieces of their lives—with my camera, with my words, in my memories. This photo to me was a classic picture of my life with girls. Aemilia and Abby, at play. On this day they were dressing up and putting on a dance routine. Their voices were raised, excited—they were directing each other, and smiling. Dressed in what they thought was pretty—was appropriate, carefully choosing their music, their audience—a singular delight to watch them. Standing by a window, a cluttered table as their background, with an audience of two, it mattered not to them—for to them it was akin to being on a grand stage, surrounded by adoring fans. It's the fairy dust of childhood that I am privileged to see. Love being mom to girls. Precious precocious adorable little critters that they are.

PUPPY LOVE (on opposite page) by Elsie Flannigan
SUPPLIES Textured cardstock: Bazzill Basics Paper; Patterned papers: Scenic Route Paper Co.; Wild Asparagus, My Mind's Eye; Flowers: Prima; Rub-ons and epoxy stickers: Autumn Leaves; Acrylic paint: Making Memories.

HOUSE OF GIRLS by Joy Bohon
SUPPLIES Patterned papers: Mustard Moon; Foam stamps, tag, bottle cap and rub-on letters: Li'l Davis Designs; Stamping ink: All Night Media; Computer font: Casablanca Antique, downloaded from the Internet; Other: Ribbon.

ALWAYS LEARNING by Maria Grace Abuzman
SUPPLIES Textured cardstock: Bazzill Basics Paper; Patterned papers: Fontwerks; Rub-ons: Fontwerks, Li'l Davis Designs and Creative Imaginations; Sticker: foof-a-La, Autumn Leaves; Pen: Pigma Micron, Sakura.

reading is my favorite way to pass the time. i remember when i was a kid, how much i'd want a new book over new clothes. and my parents cultivated my love of stories and words. i deeply appreciate them for this and the fact that i still get excited over experiencing worlds beyond my own.

challenge #3

Customize a Ribbon Border

No matter how you turn it or what you add to it (think buttons, lace, eyelets and embroidery floss), ribbon is a terrific page border that can be attached in so many creative ways—with eyelets, brads, staples, embroidery floss and more. Make sure you check out Challenge 52, where I give you clever ideas for making your own ribbon!

TRICK OR TREAT LOVE by Elsie Flannigan

SUPPLIES Patterned papers: American Crafts and KI Memories; Ribbon: Doodlebug Design and C.M. Offray & Son; Rub-ons: Li'l Davis Designs; Acrylic paint: Making Memories; Other: Thread and staples.

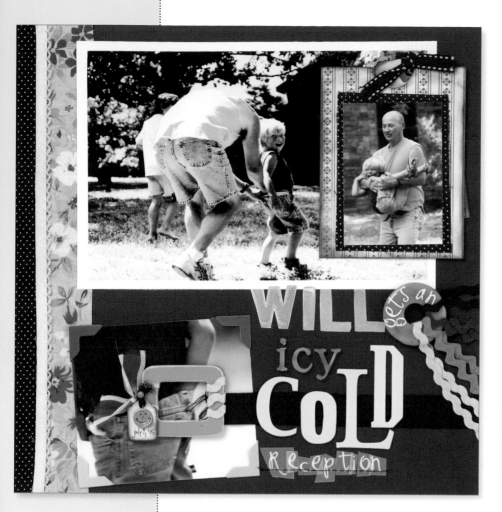

ICY COLD RECEPTION by Kendra McCracken

SUPPLIES Textured cardstock: Bazzill Basics Paper; Patterned papers: Foof-a-La, Autumn Leaves, Wooden frame. Chatterbox, Photo corners and chipboard letters: Heidi Swapp for Advantus; Rub-ons and brads: Making Memories; Acrylic letters: Paper Studio; Foam stamps: Duncan Enterprises; Ribbon: May Arts and C.M. Offray & Son; Other: Rickrack, fabric, acrylic jewelry, shipping tag and twill tape.

LAUREN by Danielle Donaldson

SUPPLIES Patterned papers: Deluxe Designs and KI Memories; Brads and staples: Making Memories; Flowers: Prima and Making Memories; Pens: EK Success, Stampin' Up! and American Crafts; Stamping ink: Stampin' Up! and Ranger Industries; Watercolors: Winsor & Newton; Carving blocks for letters: Mastercarve Blocks, Staedtler; Ribbon: May Arts.

Make Your Own: Chipboard Accents

Chipboard is so popular right now! By making your own chipboard accents, you can add a custom look to any scrapbook page. Follow the easy steps at right to make your own chipboard accent.

UNHIDDEN BEAUTY by Kendra McCracken

SUPPLIES *Textured cardstock:* Bazzill Basics Paper; *Brads and jump rings:* Junkitz; *Clear letters:* Heidi Swapp for Advantus; *Canvas label:* 7gypsies; *Rubber stamps:* PSX Design, Duncan Enterprises and unknown; *Stamping ink:* StazOn, Tsukineko; Fluid Chalk, Clearsnap; *Ribbon:* C.M. Offray & Son; *Embroidery floss:* DMC; *Other:* Acrylic paint, flowers, buttons, fabric and rhinestones.

Chipboard samples by Elsie Flannigan

step-by-step

Make Your Own: Chipboard Accents

1. Draw or trace a shape on plain chipboard.

2. Cut the accent out with scissors or a craft knife.

3. Paint the accent a fun color.

Add Details

Try buttons, flowers, stickers, jewels … anything that appeals to you!

challenge #5

Embellish a Floral Accent

No matter what your page topic, I bet you can find a place for a flower accent in your design. But take it up a notch. Embellish the center of your flower with a mini clock, a tiny thread-tied button or patterned paper. And don't be afraid to turn a large flower shape into a photo frame!

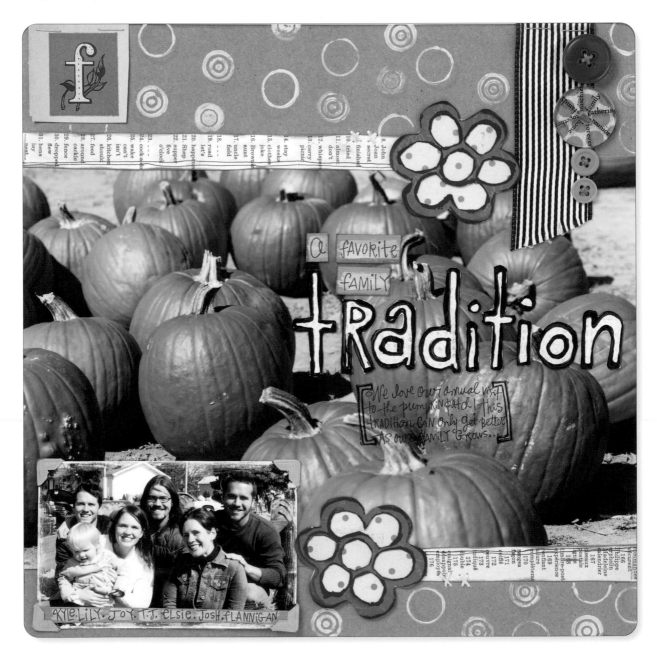

TRADITION (on opposite page) by Elsie Flannigan

SUPPLIES Textured cardstock: Bazzill Basics Paper; Patterned papers: Autumn Leaves, Scenic Route Paper Co., 7gypsies and BasicGrey; Rubber stamps: Hero Arts; Acrylic paint: Making Memories; Photo corners: Canson; Clear buttons: Junkitz; Rub-ons: 7gypsies; Other: Fabric paint, "F" monogram, buttons, thread and ribbon.

YOUR SPIRIT BLOOMS by Danielle Thompson

SUPPLIES Patterned papers: Scrapworks, Autumn Leaves, BasicGrey and Sassafras Lass; Letter stickers: BasicGrey; Rub-ons: KI Memories and BasicGrey; Flowers: Prima; Mini brads: Making Memories; Pens: Zig Writers, EK Success; Decorative-edge scissors: Provo Craft; Chalk: Craf-T Products; Computer font: 2Peas Flower Garden, downloaded from www.twopeasinabucket.com.

EVOLUTION OF LOVE by Vicki Harvey

SUPPLIES Patterned papers: Daisy D's Paper Co., Melissa Frances, Scenic Route Paper Co. and Making Memories; Chipboard letters: Heidi Swapp for Advantus; Script letter stickers: Mustard Moon; Rub-on letters: 7gypsies; Black lace: Europa Imports; Flowers: Michaels; Watch face: Li'l Davis Designs; Label holders and buttons: Making Memories; Rubber stamp: Limited Edition Rubberstamps; Acrylic paint: Delta Technical Coatings; Pink wooden heart: Over the Moon Press, EK Success; Metal photo corner: Daisy D's Paper Co.; Brads: Creative Impressions; Computer fonts: Bickley Script and Teletype, downloaded from the Internet.

Create a Ribbon Cluster

Ribbons are beautiful accents on a page—no matter what! But why not take the next step? Challenge yourself to create an accent with a cluster of ribbons. Just tie two, three, four or more ribbons and cluster them together in the same area on your page. To finish the look, tie them onto cardstock, weave them through an embroidered border, or hook a tiny safety pin through them.

Living, Loving, growing, Learning,
trying, taking chances, making mistakes
Being together, despite all odds...

T.J and ELSIE
FLANNIGAN

ONE FAMILY
ONE FRENDSHIP
ONE LOVE

DRAWING BY:
DOREN CHAPMAN

FOUR YEARS
[and Counting...]

I seriously CANNOT believe
that we are about to celebrate our
4th wedding anniversary! These past few
years have been a crazy blur! And I
are so thankful we have each other
to share this journey with! I always want
to remember how blessed we are to be together!

CUTIE (on opposite page) by Elsie Flannigan

SUPPLIES Textured cardstock: Bazzill Basics Paper; Patterned papers: Chatterbox, Making Memories, American Crafts and My Mind's Eye; Chipboard letters: Li'l Davis Designs; Brads: Making Memories, Doodlebug Design and American Crafts; Ribbon: Maya Road and Doodlebug Design; Other: Thread.

FOUR YEARS by Elsie Flannigan

SUPPLIES Textured cardstock: Bazzill Basics Paper; Patterned papers: Autumn Leaves; Chloe's Closet, Imagination Project; Rub-ons: Making Memories; Foam stamp: Li'l Davis Designs; Ribbon: Doodlebug Design; Flower: Prima; Other: Buttons and thread.

PIERCINGLY GREAT! by Julie Scattaregia

SUPPLIES Patterned paper, foam stamps, chipboard frame, rub-ons and safety pin: Li'l Davis Designs; Acrylic paint, flowers, brads, rub-ons and small photo turn: Making Memories; Decorative rub-on: Scrapperware, Creative Imaginations; Large photo turns: 7gypsies; Ribbon: Narratives, Creative Imaginations; C.M. Offray & Son; Metal corner on frame: Embellish It!; Other: Heart charm.

PIERCINGLY GREAT

OFFICIALLY IRRESISTIBLE OFFICIALLY

You could hardly wait for your eighth birthday! It was ear-piercing day!
You practically ran through the door at Claires, plopped right into the ear
piercing chair, and excitedly began looking at all of the earring choices.
You were doing really great, until…you saw it. The ear piercing gun.
At that exact moment, you grabbed your ears and made a scared, yet
hilarious face. After that, you put on your brave face, toughed out the
pain, and sported your new "diamond" earrings home. Way to go, Alexa!

turning 8

Take an Artistic Photograph

It's easy to capture photographs of family and events. But for this challenge, I want you to look through the lens of your camera as a photo enthusiast. Take a closer glance at things in your life that you might otherwise walk on by. Look for beauty in unexpected places, inside and outside of your home!

HOSPITALITY

We stayed at my grandma's last month. In the room we slept in we found this sweet little stack of wash cloths. I was so touched by this simple, thoughtful act of hospitality. These things make me feel loved. This is how I always want our home to feel... ♡

HOSPITALITY (on opposite page)
by Elsie Flannigan

SUPPLIES Textured cardstock: Bazzill Basics Paper; Patterned papers: Scenic Route Paper Co.; Chipboard and photo corner: Heidi Swapp for Advantus; Flowers: Prima; Tabs: Autumn Leaves.

FOUR YEARS AGO by Joy Bohon

SUPPLIES Patterned papers: Karen Foster Design and Scenic Route Paper Co.; Transparency: 3M; Epoxy letters, bookplates, rub-ons and plastic number: Li'l Davis Designs; Large rub-on letters and brads: Making Memories; Stamping ink: All Night Media; Computer font: Butterbrotpapier, downloaded from the Internet.

LIFE HAPPENS by Maria Grace Abuzman

SUPPLIES Patterned paper: Christina Cole for Provo Craft; Rub-ons: Making Memories; Ribbon: Strano Designs; Stamping ink: ColorBox, Clearsnap; Label: Chronicle Books; Pen: Pigma Micron, Sakura; Other: Notebook paper.

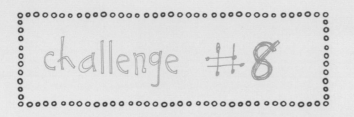

challenge #8

Group Four Photos

I love creating one-photo layouts, but sometimes I have more than one photograph to feature on a page. I like to take four (or more) photographs and cluster them together in a group. This makes them appear almost as one large focal-point photo but allows me to display more images at one time. Try it!

One of the best things in the world to be is a boy; it requires no experience, but needs some practice to be a good one. —Charles Dudley Warner

T.J., Tom and Josh ☆ Spring '05

boxing boys

Such good Memories! In the fall of '98 and '99 [my] Sophomore And Junior Years Sara, Josh, Nik and I went to Indiana for a Christian Music Fest for a Weekend! Sara's parents took us in there RV and we had So Much fun, feeling like Miss Angie, Plumb And Chasing Furies, Camping, Making frozen Pizza, Swimming, Dancing And PLAYING twenty Questions! Josh and Nik got matching snow caps And Sara And I tried to be all domestic And make ourb DINNER Super Cute ☺ We made a fire and took walks together and just hung out. The first Year we went Josh And Nik got to meet Miss Angie [my Hero at the time] and Sara and I totally freaked out and were so jealous ♡♡ these times I spent with our group of friends were so totally precious And I want to always remember them but is fun looking back at this six years later, we are all married And they all have a BABY too? Fun Memories. Fun times, things I will keep in my heart ♡journaling '05

98 and 99

BOXING BOYS (on opposite page) by Elsie Flannigan

SUPPLIES Textured cardstock: Bazzill Basics Paper; Ribbon, quote sticker and patterned papers: KI Memories; Foam stamps: Li'l Davis Designs; Brad and epoxy accents: Autumn Leaves.

FUN MEMORIES by Elsie Flannigan

SUPPLIES Patterned papers: Provo Craft and Scenic Route Paper Co.; Rub-ons: Making Memories and KI Memories; Acrylic paint: Making Memories.

9 YEARS by Elsie Flannigan

SUPPLIES Cardstock, sticker and rub-ons: Making Memories; Patterned paper: Die Cuts With a View; Tag: KI Memories; Chipboard: Heidi Swapp for Advantus; Other: Buttons and thread.

97

98

2000

02

04

T.J. And Elsie. We Are Growing, Learning, Loving, Working And Enjoying this Journey

Life began after I fell in love with you. -B. Hodge

99

01

03

05

9 YEARS... wow. 9 years since we fell in love. I always knew we were soul mates. That is an amazing feeling! Each Year Each Memory is A treasure And A blessing! This is our story, the story of TJ And Elsie ♡

Doodle on Photographs

Don't be afraid to express yourself by doodling right on your photos! (If you're worried about ruining them, doodle on a digital print.) Try using your own handwriting in an open area of the photograph—or use a doodled rub-on instead!

AT 21 by Elsie Flannigan

SUPPLIES Textured cardstock: Bazzill Basics Paper; Rub-ons, stickers and acrylic accents: KI Memories; Twill tape: 7gypsies; Epoxy stickers: Christina Cole for Provo Craft; Brad and pen: American Crafts.

DREAMING by Elsie Flannigan

SUPPLIES Textured cardstock: Bazzill Basics Paper; Patterned paper and stickers: Chatterbox; Ribbon: C.M. Offray & Son and American Crafts; Pen: Slick Writer, American Crafts; Other: Flower, ribbon and jute.

ALEX ON YOUR SHOULDER MAKES YOU HAPPY
by Joy Bohon

SUPPLIES Textured cardstock: KI Memories; Patterned paper: Scrapworks; Rub-on hearts: KI Memories; Rub-on text: 7gypsies; Acetate hearts: Heidi Swapp for Advantus; Letter stickers: American Crafts; Computer fonts: Mechanical Fun, downloaded from the Internet; AL Uncle Charles, downloaded from www.twopeasinabucket.com; Other: Staples.

challenge #10

Mini Album: Be Real

Julie Scattaregia came up with this great journaling idea. Here's the challenge in her own words: "I'm a blogger wannabe. But the time and energy associated with the upkeep of a site seems too daunting for me right now. So, I consider this journal to be a place like my blog. I don't make daily entries, but it's a place where I can record some of the 'real' stuff in life. Some serious, some funny, some not so funny. But all of it real!"

BE YOURSELF by Julie Scattaregia

SUPPLIES Chipboard album, chipboard letters and coasters, and ribbon: Li'l Davis Designs; Patterned papers and letter stickers: BasicGrey; Tabs and negative strip: Narratives, Creative Imaginations; Rub-ons: Daisy D's Paper Co. and Making Memories; Rub-ons: Scrapperware, Creative Imaginations; Ribbon: C.M. Offray & Son; Rubber stamps: Hampton Art Stamps, Nostalgiques and Postmodern Design; "Time" concho and photo turn: 7gypsies; Stamping ink: StazOn, Tsukineko; Label tape: Dymo; Other: Silk flowers.

I'm a blogger wannabe. It's true. But I know me. Maintaining a blog site would be the emotional equivalent of giving up chocolate. In other words, "It ain't gonna happen." I like my M&M's entirely too much. And not just the pretty, dainty ones. We're talking "Mega M&M's." The kind on steroids with a promise of serious water retention. So, until I can look chocolate straight in the eye and say with conviction, "I don't love you. I've never loved you!," I'll continue to get my blogger's fix by lurking on the sites of my seriously talented friends. And I plan to let this journal serve as my surrogate blog. Less maintenance and more chocolate. Works for me!

FUNNY

JS

THOUGHTS ON GROWING older

Smile lines. Schmile lines. Nothing about them makes me smile. Oh, don't get me wrong. I'm not submitting my photo to Willard Scott for placement on a Smucker's jar any time soon.

But things are a changin'! If only I had understood the adverse affect of smearing half a bottle of baby oil on my face then baking in the scorching sun for hours. Ouch! It hurts just thinking about it. Yes, with age comes wisdom.

But why do these uninvited wrinkles feel the need to tag along? Age gracefully? Perhaps. Age quietly? Not by the hair of my chinny, chin, chin! Well, at least I don't have that to worry about…yet…

TIME

FUNNY

challenge #10

Mini Album: Be Real continued

happiness

HAPPINESS

It's not just a cliché. I'm happy. There. I said it. And I won't apologize for it. Oh, sure I have my moments. Just ask my kids! But, gone are the days of being a people pleaser, and I'm a happier girl because of it. Sure, I still care what other people think. But I don't dwell on it. I no longer need their approval. Instead, I look to the ones who really matter in my life. Christ covers me with grace and gives me joy. I have a husband who loves me and accepts my imperfections. And get this, my kids still think I'm a pretty cool Mom (I'll enjoy that one while it lasts!). A perfect life? Puhleeeease! I'm just a girl who is never too old to learn!

Buy stock in Bandaids.

Forgive quickly. Forgive completely.

The sooner I let go of the bike, the quicker they'll learn to ride!

My favorite color is brown.

Trips to the dollar store are just as exciting as trips to Nordstroms.

Hopscotch and jump-rope will never go out of style.

REMEMBER

Some Life Lessons

that I've learned from the kids.

Quiz #1

What's Your Perfect Scrapbooking Retreat?

Whether you scrapbook at your kitchen table or have a whole room dedicated to your favorite hobby, I'll bet you sometimes dream about the perfect scrapbooking getaway! This "just-for-fun" quiz will point you in the right direction! Have fun with it (and think about how you might be able to use these answers to create a really cool scrapbook page!).

Which color combination grabs your attention first?

a. Blue, green, sand dollar

b. Black, white, gold

c. Rose, green, ivory

d. Turquoise, red, orange

You'd buy a bracelet made from:

a. Seashells

b. Faux jewels

c. Pretty floral ribbons

d. Handmade beads

If you could photograph anything in the world, you'd choose:

a. A sandy beach, with ocean waves crashing to the shore

b. The Eiffel Tower

c. A beautiful garden in bloom

d. A palm tree

You'd choose a side-table made from:

a. Distressed wood

b. Wrought iron

c. Hammered brass

d. Bamboo

Your favorite fabric is:

a. Breezy cotton

b. Silk brocade

c. Floral chintz

d. A handwoven textile

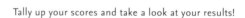

Tally up your scores and take a look at your results!

If you answered mostly "A," then your perfect scrapbooking weekend would take place at a coastal retreat. Imagine waking up in the morning and taking a walk along the beach, scrapbooking all afternoon, and then dining at the little seafood restaurant down the way that all the locals rave about!

If you answered mostly "B," then your perfect scrapbooking weekend would take place in a Paris apartment. Think classy, elegant, stress-free and relaxing all at the same time. Soak up the beautiful atmosphere as you transfer it to your scrapbook pages!

If you answered mostly "C," then your perfect scrapbooking weekend would take place in a little country cottage. Imagine being surrounded by beautiful gardens and scrapbooking in a cozy little space filled with floral prints and time-worn furniture!

If you answered mostly "D," then your perfect scrapbooking weekend would take place in a tropical setting. Think of the inspiration you'd draw from the brightly colored sunsets, the tropical breezes and the cute little umbrellas tucked into those yummy pineapple-inspired drinks!

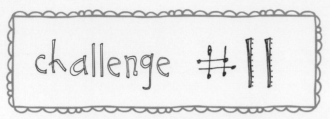

challenge #11

Scraplift a Color Combination

I loved the blues, browns and oranges on Mellette's layout, so I decided to scraplift her color combination for my pages at right. For this challenge, you can scraplift me—or Mellette—or open up this book to any page and challenge yourself to scraplift the color scheme!

You are **pure potential,** son. In your eyes I see so much love, kindness, and the ability to do remarkable things.

PURE POTENTIAL (on opposite page) by Mellette Berezoski

SUPPLIES Patterned papers: Wild Asparagus, My Mind's Eye; Déjà Views, The C-Thru Ruler Co.; Scenic Route Paper Co.; BasicGrey; Making Memories; Coin mounts: Whitman; Metal frame, metal word charm, screw-top eyelets, circle cutter and floss: Making Memories; Ribbon: Making Memories and May Arts; Photo corner: Heidi Swapp for Advantus; Computer font: AL Songwriter, downloaded from www.twopeasinabucket.com; Times New Roman, Microsoft Word.

10 THINGS I LOVE by Elsie Flannigan

SUPPLIES Textured cardstock: Bazzill Basics Paper; Patterned papers, stickers, tags and acrylic accents: KI Memories; Photo corners: Canson and Heidi Swapp for Advantus; Letter sticker: American Crafts; Other: Buttons and thread.

SOULMATES by Elsie Flannigan

SUPPLIES Embroidery Floss: DMC; Circle Punch: EK Success.

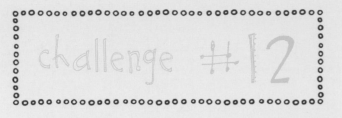
Scraplift a Layout Shape

Danielle wanted this sun-shaped page to have an artsy, vibrant, funky feel to it. I love the high energy of her layout and decided to scraplift it. My layout isn't an exact sun shape, but look how I've started with a circle shape and then added ribbons and different patterns around the perimeter of my circle. For this challenge, look for a layout with a shape you love and challenge yourself to scraplift it!

EMANATE (on opposite page) by Danielle Thompson

SUPPLIES Rhinestones and sequins: Westrim Crafts; Pens: Zig Writer, EK Success; Sakura; Chalk: Craf-T Products; Letter stickers: BasicGrey; Embroidery floss: DMC; Canvas tape: 7gypsies.

MY HEART BELONGS TO by Elsie Flannigan

SUPPLIES Textured cardstock: Bazzill Basics Paper; Patterned papers: Sakar; Chloe's Closet, Imagination Project; Christina Cole for Provo Craft; Making Memories; Rub-ons: Autumn Leaves and Fontwerks; Flowers: Prima; Brads: Bazzill Basics Paper, Making Memories, American Crafts and Doodlebug Design; Acrylic paint: Heidi Swapp for Advantus; Other: Buttons and rhinestones.

EVERYTHING IS BETTER by Elsie Flannigan

SUPPLIES Textured cardstock: Bazzill Basics Paper; Ribbon: May Arts and C.M. Offray & Son; Flowers: Prima; Other: Buttons and rhinestones.

Mini Album: Favorite Sayings

Vicki has this to say about this challenge: "We seem to have our own language in the Harvey house! Each time I talk to one of my friends on the phone, she says she can never understand what I'm saying. I decided that a dictionary with some of the terms we use in our house would be a fun thing for our guests to read. I love that this album will help me remember some of the little details of our lives now that may be lost at some point later in time."

HARVEYISMS by Vicki Harvey

SUPPLIES Patterned papers: KI Memories; Mustard Moon; Scenic Route Paper Co.; Scrapworks; Melissa Frances; foof-a-La, Autumn Leaves; Chatterbox; Daisy D's Paper Co.; Letter stickers: American Crafts, Making Memories and Scenic Route Paper Co.; Rub-ons: Scenic Route Paper Co. and 7gypsies; Zigzag-stitch stamp: Hero Arts; Stamping ink: Stampin' Up!; Ticket: MMF Industries; Label tape: Dymo; Picture hanger: Daisy D's Paper Co.; Twill: Scenic Route Paper Co.; Fabric tab: Scrapworks; Photo corners: Chatterbox, Kolo and Waste Not Paper; Brads: Heidi Swapp for Advantus; Brown rickrack: Wrights; Ribbon: Li'l Davis Designs, Morex and May Arts; Index-file cards and loose-leaf rings: Office Depot; Computer fonts: Avant Garde, Microsoft Word; Garamouche, downloaded from the Internet; Other: Staples.

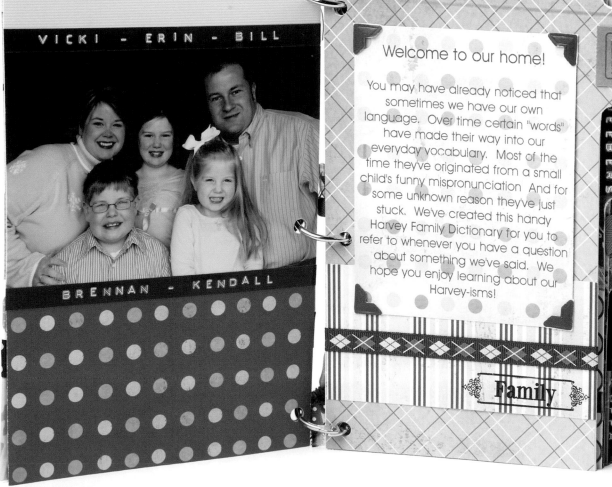

VICKI - ERIN - BILL

BRENNAN - KENDALL

Welcome to our home!

You may have already noticed that sometimes we have our own language. Over time certain "words" have made their way into our everyday vocabulary. Most of the time they've originated from a small child's funny mispronunciation. And for some unknown reason they've just stuck. We've created this handy Harvey Family Dictionary for you to refer to whenever you have a question about something we've said. We hope you enjoy learning about our Harvey-isms!

Family

OOEY GOOEY

5

Mini Album: Favorite Sayings continued

SEBASTIAN JOE'S

MINNEAPOLIS, MN

THE BEST ICE CREAM IN THE WORLD

sweet

RASPBERRY CHOCOLATE CHIP

Sweet

OOEY GOOEY

ooey gooey ($\overline{oo} \cdot \bar{e}$ $g\overline{oo} \cdot \bar{e}$) 1. any type of sweet, delicious dessert. 2. what Bill brings home to Vicki when she has PMS.

Bumpie

family FUN

Bumpie (bum·pē) 1. Grandpa Jim 2. An amazing man. 3. What Erin has called Grandpa since she was a baby and couldn't say Grampie. 4. The word adopted by our entire family to denote this man.

challenge #14

Scraplift a Technique

Vicki's layout inspired me to take out my sewing machine and sew a simple stitched frame around the focal point of my layout. Even though our layouts are actually quite different, they show how one technique can be adapted to any design.

erin

pre teen

january 2005

caught between...

little girl and young lady

an eternity for you

just the blink of an eye for me

POSH

PUPPY!!

HOT STUFF

Don't treat me any differently than you would the Queen

Happiness is a closet full of cute clothes.

cocoa

O.K, i Admit it! our puppy cocoa is a little posh♥... She hAs tons of cute clothes (yes, even Accessories!). And she even hAs some outfits thAt Are custom mAde (SHHH!) ☺

PRE-TEEN (on opposite page) by Vicki Harvey

SUPPLIES Patterned papers: Chatterbox; Red chipboard letters, flower and index tabs: Heidi Swapp for Advantus; Pink chipboard letter squares and button: Making Memories; Ribbon: C.M. Offray & Son; Lace: Europa Imports; Embroidery floss: DMC; Computer font: Avant Garde, Microsoft Word.

POSH PUPPY by Elsie Flannigan

SUPPLIES Patterned papers, ribbon, transparency and stickers: KI Memories; Large letter stickers: Gin-X, Imagination Project.

MOMENTS LIKE THESE by Elsie Flannigan

SUPPLIES Patterned paper: Chloe's Closet, Imagination Project; Ribbon: American Crafts and Doodlebug Design; Pen: Sakura; Acrylic paint: Making Memories; Computer font: 2Peas Flower Garden, downloaded from www.twopeasinabucket.com; Other: Staples, buttons, thread and chalk.

moments like these make life rich.

challenge #15

Scraplift a Layout Idea

I scraplifted several components from Joy's page. I loved how she combined a card-stock background with bright, bold colors and how she journaled on strips of paper. But what really caught my eye was how she positioned elements right off her page. I love how the circles extend beyond the scope of her background. Take a peek, too, at how Maria Grace scraplifted Joy's design by allowing her photograph to skim past the edge of the page. I can't wait to see your take on this challenge!

SuN

Sweet summer fun

Loving the water

Loving the warmth

Totally oblivious

Unconcerned

Time passes in a void

Supreme cuteness

In your little bikini

With smiles galore

Fighting over goggles

with your sister

Perfect moments

Perfect days

Miss petite perfection

My aemilia summer 05

WHEN
YOU
KNOW...

[Life is Pretty Sweet!]

everything hopes for a year or so

God chas blessed you.

You are living your dreams.

You are with your Soul Mate.

You Have found a Safe place.

You are married to your best friend.

You have a lot to Look forward to.

SUN by Joy Bohon

SUPPLIES Textured cardstock: Bazzill Basics Paper and KI Memories; Patterned paper, letter sticker, epoxy letters and ribbon sticker: Li'l Davis Designs; Epoxy circles: MOD, Autumn Leaves; Metal letters: American Crafts; Computer font: 2Peas Weathered Fence, downloaded from www.twopeasinabucket.com.

WHEN YOU KNOW by Elsie Flannigan

SUPPLIES Textured cardstock: Bazzill Basics Paper; Foam stamps: Li'l Davis Designs; Acrylic paint: Making Memories and Heidi Swapp for Advantus; Pens: Sakura; Ribbon: Doodlebug Design, Flair Designs and May Arts.

YOU'VE LEFT AN IMPRESSION
by Maria Grace Abuzman

SUPPLIES Textured cardstock: Bazzill Basics Paper; Letter stamps, rub-on letters and image stamp: Fontwerks; Rub-ons: Heidi Swapp for Advantus; Acrylic paint: Liquitex; Stamping ink: Ranger Industries and Tsukineko; Pen: Pigma Micron, Sakura; Labels: Chronicle Books.

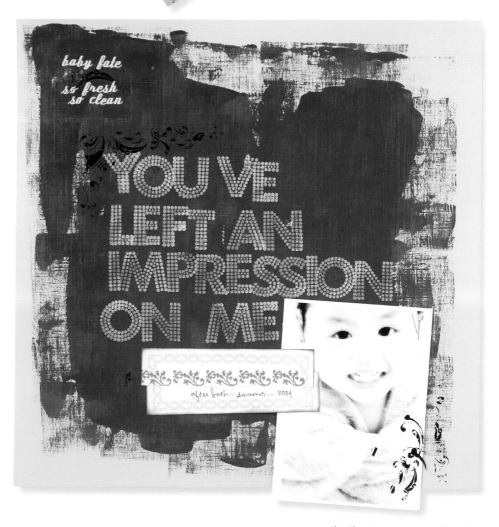

baby fate
so fresh
so clean

YOU'VE
LEFT AN
IMPRESSION
ON ME

after bath... summer... 2004

Scraplift a Topic

Rachel's layout about how her camera is her baby inspired me to scrapbook about my camera, too. I really love the shot of Rachel holding her camera and the way she layered those open letters right over her photograph.

my camera is aka baby* no.two (soon to be no. three)

a bit of a running joke in our house, but oh so true. i love my camera. a lot.

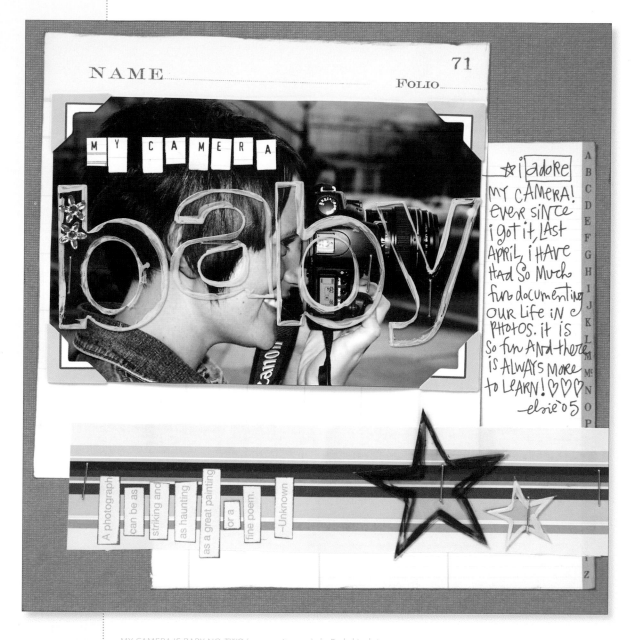

NAME _____ 71

FOLIO _____

MY CAMERA

baby

☆i adore MY CAMERA! ever since i got it, last APRIL, i have had So Much fun documenting our life in e photos. it is So fun And there is ALWAYS More to LEARN! ♡♡♡
—elsie`05

A photograph / can be as / striking and / as haunting / as a great painting / or a / fine poem. / —Unknown

MY CAMERA IS BABY NO. TWO (on opposite page) by Rachel Ludwig
SUPPLIES Textured cardstock: Bazzill Basics Paper; Letter stickers: Marcella by Kay; Fabric letters: Scrapworks; Rub-ons: Scrapworks and Fontwerks; Letter stamps: Fontwerks; Stamping ink: Nick Bantock, Ranger Industries.

MY CAMERA BABY by Elsie Flannigan
SUPPLIES Textured cardstock: Die Cuts With a View; Patterned paper: Making Memories; Acetate letters and shapes, photo tape, flower jewels, photo corners and acrylic paint: Heidi Swapp for Advantus; Tabs: Autumn Leaves; Quote sticker: KI Memories.

elsie's box

{ As a scrapbooker, you may want to create a page about how you love your camera—or maybe you just want to flip through the pages of Creating Keepsakes and find a topic that inspires you! What layout topics reach out and grab your attention? }

challenge #17

Scraplift an Alphabetical Approach

I love how Julie used so many different types of letters on her page. I also love how she customized them to fit her personal style. Experiment with letters on a scrapbook page—and make them your own by embellishing them in a way that suits your scrapbooking personality!

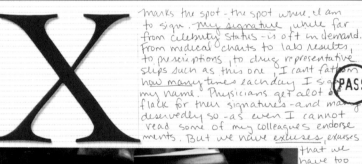

ALEXA (on opposite page) by Julie Scattaregia

SUPPLIES Patterned papers: Scenic Route Paper Co.; Foam stamp, letters, wooden flowers, rub-ons and paper clip: Li'l Davis Designs; Chipboard letter, rub-ons and metal screen: Making Memories; File folder and photo turn: 7gypsies; Twill and rub-ons: Creative Imaginations; Wooden frame: Chatterbox; Acrylic paint: Delta Technical Coatings; Ribbon: C.M. Offray & Son; Label tape: Dymo.

E IS FOR ELSIE by Elsie Flannigan

SUPPLIES Textured cardstock: KI Memories; Patterned papers: Chatterbox; Chloe's Closet, Imagination Project; Letter stickers: KI Memories, American Crafts and Gin-X, Imagination Project; Metal letters: American Crafts; Ribbon and quote sticker: KI Memories; Other: Felt and thread.

X by Joy Bohon

SUPPLIES Patterned paper: Scrapworks; Chipboard letter: Heidi Swapp for Advantus; Acrylic paint and rub-on tags: Making Memories; Rub-on letters: Autumn Leaves; Pen: American Crafts.

X marks the spot - the spot where I am to sign. My signature, while far from celebrity status - is oft in demand. From medical charts to lab results, to prescriptions, to drug representative slips such as this one, I can't fathom how many times each day I sign my name. Physicians get a lot of flack for their signatures - and many deservedly so - as even I cannot read some of my colleagues endorsements. But we have excuses, excuses that we have too much to do, too little time to do it in, and too many slips to sign. My own hand writing has deteriorated with time, with use. It is mine, it identifies me, my work. It speaks of my attention to those papers I have signed, it carries more weight than I ever thought it would. Never special to begin with, now tempered with time, with use - it is sad but not lonely. And despite its natural destruction over time, its wearing away - I think I still have held to my promise to myself that it shall always be legible in my work. [Not perfect - Not beautiful - just legible] And that folks - is my X one the spot. Joy Bohon MD

X ___ X ___ X ___ X ___ X

Challenge #18

Scraplift a Page Design

I like to challenge myself by pushing the limits of what a scrapbook page can be. Mary Grace reminded me that blank space on a layout can be super effective. Do you see where I scraplifted three of her ideas? Take a look at how I created a block on my page and journaled about something I love, and check out our similar color schemes.

elsie's box

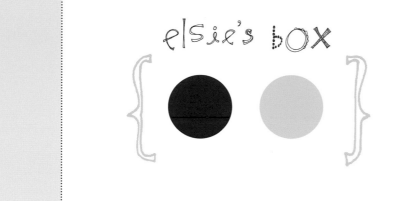

AND IN THIS CORNER (on opposite page)
by Mary Grace Abuzman

SUPPLIES Textured cardstock: Die Cuts With a View and Making Memories; Patterned paper and rub-ons: Fontwerks, Ribbon: Boxer Scrapbook Productions; Stamping ink: ColorBox, Clearsnap; Pen: Pigma Micron, Sakura; Photo corners: Kolo.

BEAUTIFUL THINGS by Elsie Flannigan

SUPPLIES Patterned papers, tag, quote sticker and flower: KI Memories; Rubber stamp: Hero Arts; Stamping ink: ColorBox, Clearsnap; Twill tape: 7gypsies; Other: Ribbon, staples and embossed paper.

challenge #19

Scraplift a Layout Shape

There are so many ways to scraplift! I hope this challenge will give you yet another approach to take when reading your scrapbooking magazines for ideas. Here, I scraplifted the basic shape of Kendra's layout.

elsie's box

I always like to sketch layouts that catch my eye. Here's my sketch of Kendra's layout and of my layout so you easily see my scraplift!

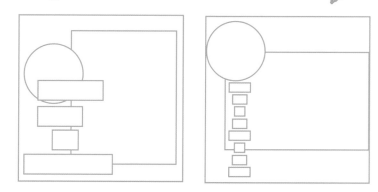

SPINNING OUT OF CONTROL (on opposite page) by Kendra McCracken

SUPPLIES Textured cardstock: Bazzill Basics Paper, Colorbök and unknown; Patterned paper, photo anchors, loose-leaf rings, jump rings and long brads: Junkitz; Chipboard stars: Making Memories; Rub-ons and rubber stamps: Fontwerks; Label tape: Dymo; Ribbon: C.M. Offray & Son and unknown; Stamping ink: Stampabilities; Computer font: 8 Track, downloaded from www.dafont.com.

MY TWIN by Elsie Flannigan

SUPPLIES Patterned papers: Chloe's Closet, Imagination Project; Scenic Route Paper Co.; KI Memories; Ribbon: Li'l Davis Designs; Rubber stamp: Fontwerks, Acrylic paint: Making Memories; Other: Button and thread.

challenge #20

Make Your Own: Patterned Paper

You can add your own unique style to your layouts in so many ways. One of my favorites? Making my own patterned paper. From making patterns with paint to using your computer to create a digital design, you can take so many different approaches. And it's easy! Here's how.

TROUBLE by Traci Turchin
SUPPLIES Software: Adobe Photoshop CS; Computer font: Univers; Stamp: A Muse Artstamps.

Patterned paper samples at right by Elsie Flannigan

step-by-step

Make Your Own: Patterned Paper

1. Sketch a design in pencil on plain white paper.

2. Paint the design with fun colors you love.

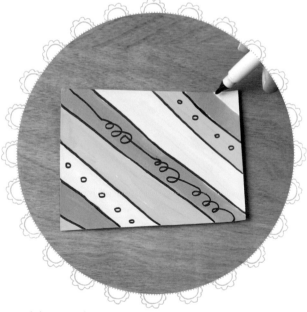

Add Details

You can outline the shapes with a pen, sew on the paper or add stamped images. Be creative and try several different options—it will get you excited to create more!

challenge #21

Mini Album: Cute Tin

The photo of Danielle's daughter and niece inspired her to create this cute mini album. The girls are at an age when you can still see the child in them but also get a glimpse of what's to come. Danielle wanted her photographs to have a worn, soft effect, so she used Photoshop to desaturate them. She adhered the photos to her pages first and then pieced patterned paper around them. To finish, she added strong black lettering and funky rub-ons, and colored her doodles with watercolor crayons to add a fun punch of color.

SURFER GIRLS by Danielle Donaldson

SUPPLIES Patterned papers, rub-ons and acrylic frame: KI Memories; Stamping ink: Stampin' Up!; Sequins: Doodlebug Design; Staples: Making Memories; Pens: EK Success, Stampin' Up! and American Crafts; Flowers: Prima; Ribbon: American Crafts and May Arts; Tin: Autumn Leaves; Other: Beads.

Michelle decided to teach Lauren how to surf this summer... they only managed to get her up once...

catch a wave

...(sorta)

digging for crabs they're FAST!! clay and the girls

San diego. Ca

august. 05

surfer girls

challenge #21

Mini Album: Cute Tin continued

Quiz #2

What's Your Favorite Place to Find Inspiration?

Scrapbooking inspiration is everywhere. I love taking my little notebook with me and jotting down ideas when I'm out and about. This little "just-for-fun" quiz will help you target your best place to look for scrapbooking inspiration at this very moment in time. But they're all fun ideas, so be sure to try each one!

Which word describes how you feel at this very moment?

a. Crazy
b. Dedicated
c. Resourceful
d. Peaceful

If you're not scrapbooking, you're probably:

a. Working out
b. Chasing after the kids
c. Cooking a gourmet meal
d. Watching television

Your favorite day of the week is:

a. Monday
b. Friday
c. Saturday
d. Sunday

Friends would call you:

a. Outgoing
b. Happy
c. Artistic
d. Good-natured

One of your goals in life is to:

a. Be published
b. Be happy
c. Be creative
d. Be relaxed

Tally up your answers and take a peek at your results!

If you answered mostly "A," you're feeling energetic and ready for something a little bit out of the ordinary. Grab a map of your hometown and find a store or a restaurant that you've never been to before. Now … go! Look around with searching eyes for a spectacular piece of inspiration that might make your next page a real stand-out!

If you answered mostly "B," you're already optimistic that you'll find a great new source of inspiration for scrapbooking your family today. Hey, if you've got kids, load them up in the car and look for scrapbooking inspiration in a kid-themed place, like a play place at a local restaurant or a mini-golf course. Use your good sense of humor and witty outlook to discover an unexpected scrapbooking surprise!

If you answered mostly "C," I'm sure you're ready to go and create—with something you've never tried before. Hmmm, an artist doesn't have to just use a paintbrush with paints … how about painting with those chopsticks from the Chinese food restaurant or incorporating the words on your fortune into a layout that's all about you?

If you answered mostly "D," you're a "go with the flow" kind of gal. Balance, happiness and relaxation are all important to you. Find inspiration in a quiet walk in a beautiful place or by looking for beauty through the lens of your camera. Whatever you choose, just allow yourself to relax and enjoy.

challenge #22

Scraplift a Journaling Style

I loved how Joy started the journaling on her page with the word "free." When I look at her page, I see the word free! I decided to use a similar idea on my page, using the word "fresh." Here's your challenge: Choose one word that summarizes your layout and repeat it several times in your journaling. You'll see that it can make a powerful impact!

{ There are tons of different ways to add journaling to a page. One of my favorite ideas is to journal around the edge of a cluster of photographs. It's a fast and simple way to add both journaling and a border at the same time! }

FREE (on opposite page) by Joy Bohon
SUPPLIES *Patterned paper: Karen Foster Design; Chipboard letters, stars and acrylic paint: Heidi Swapp for Advantus; Other: Chipboard.*

FRESH by Elsie Flannigan
SUPPLIES *Textured cardstock: Bazzill Basics Paper; Patterned papers: KI Memories, Sassafras Lass, Scenic Route Paper Co. and American Crafts; Ribbon: C.M. Offray & Son and Doodlebug Design; Photo corners: Heidi Swapp for Advantus; Stickers: Making Memories; Other: Staples, button and thread.*

challenge #23

Make Your Own: Buttons

Making buttons is super easy. I made these buttons from paper clay. I cut them out with small cookie cutters and etched different designs in them with a craft knife and a pen. After they dried, I simply painted them. Here's how.

SEVEN DAYS OF BLISS
by Elsie Flannigan
SUPPLIES Patterned paper: BasicGrey; Rubber stamp: Hero Arts; Stamping ink: ColorBox, Clearsnap; Buttons: Elsie's own designs; Other: Thread and rhinestones.

Button samples by Elsie Flannigan

step-by-step

Make Your Own: Buttons

1. Roll out paper clay (you can use your hands!)

2. Cut a circle out with a small cookie cutter.

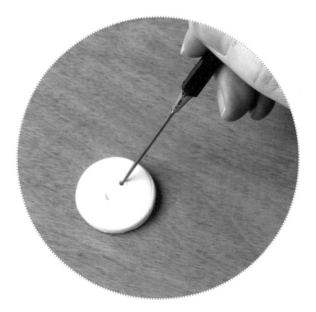

3. Add holes to the button.

Add Details

Paint the button and add details. You can use just one color, or add several colors and designs for a funky look!

challenge #24

Design with White Cardstock

Think of it like this: a plain white background is the little black dress of scrapbook pages. Always there when you need it, always simple and elegant. I sometimes forget about white cardstock, but when I saw Rachel's beautiful pages, I knew I wanted to pull it out and try it again. I love the results! Go ahead and take the challenge—see what you can create with a not-so-plain white cardstock background.

QUITE THE CATCH by Elsie Flannigan
SUPPLIES Textured cardstock: Bazzill Basics Paper; Decorative tape and rub-ons: Gin-X, Imagination Project; Brad: American Crafts; Other: Fabric paint.

man & wife

and the two shall become one...

AUGUST 13 2005

MAN & WIFE by Rachel Ludwig
SUPPLIES Textured cardstock: Bazzill Basics Paper, Fabric: Amy Butler; Photo corners: Canson; Rub-ons: Autumn Leaves; Stamping ink: ColorBox, Clearsnap; Computer font: Porcelain, downloaded from the Internet.

BIG BROTHER TO BE by Rachel Ludwig
SUPPLIES Textured cardstock: Bazzill Basics Paper; Plastic letters: KI Memories; Letter stickers: American Crafts; Photo corners: Scrapworks; Rub-ons: Fontwerks; Computer font: Myriad, Microsoft Word.

you were so excited when you found out you were finally going to be a big brother. this cool shirt allowed

BIG BROTHER TO BE

i love how this picture captures how excited you were about it all!

you to be the bearer of the exciting news to opa & oma and grandpa & grandma. you loved being part of the surprise, and played the part perfectly.

challenge #25

Album: Inspiration Journal

What better place to keep track of the things you love and are inspired by than a personalized inspiration journal? I love the approach Danielle took in her journal and how she customized it to suit her style. I'd like to challenge you to make your own inspiration journal, too—and remember, it can be any shape, size or material … whatever works for you!

CRAZY ART JOURNAL by Danielle Donaldson

SUPPLIES Patterned papers: My Mind's Eye, Autumn Leaves, Daisy D's Paper Co., Chatterbox and Rusty Pickle; Stamping ink: Ranger Industries and Stampin' Up!; Rub-ons, staples and acrylic paint: Making Memories; Letter stickers: American Crafts; Punch: EK Success; Flowers: Prima; Pens: EK Success, Stampin' Up! and American Crafts; Ribbon: May Arts, Doodlebug Design, Making Memories and Scrapworks; Quotes: From "Calvin and Hobbes" by Bill Watterson; Other: Glitter, photo corners, beaded fringe, rhinestones, fabric and binder.

challenge #25

Album: Inspiration Journal continued

Make Your Own: Clear Flower Embellishments

You'll see these clear flower embellishments blooming all over my scrapbook pages!
I love how they look, and they're so easy to make. Just follow these steps:

PLAY TOGETHER by Elsie Flannigan

SUPPLIES Textured cardstock: Bazzill Basics Paper; Stickers: Li'l Davis Designs; Epoxy accents: Autumn Leaves; Rub-ons: Fontwerks, KI Memories, Autumn Leaves and K&Company.

Flower samples by Elsie Flannigan

Make Your Own: Clear Flower Embellishments

Draw or trace a flower shape on clear plastic (like a transparency or sheet protector).

2 Cut the shape out with scissors.

Paint the edges to add definition.

Make Your Own: Clear Flower Embellishments continued

ESSENCE by Elsie Flannigan
SUPPLIES Textured cardstock: Bazzill Basics Paper; Transparency: KI Memories; Flowers: Prima; Brads: American Crafts and Doodlebug Design; Acrylic paint: Making Memories; Other: Rhinestones, fabric paint, buttons and thread.

Quiz #3

What's Your Journaling Style?

Journaling is an important element on any scrapbook page, but there's no right or wrong way to tell your story. There is only your way! You can tell your story any way you like. If you need a starting place, take this little "just-for-fun" quiz:

You want to touch base with a friend. You:

a. Call
b. Text
c. E-mail
d. Instant message

You're going out tonight. What do you wear?

a. Something trendy
b. Something casual
c. Something pretty
d. Something comfy

How many hours do you spend on the computer a day?

a. Less than one
b. 1–2
c. 3–4
d. 5 or more

You're sending a friend a birthday card. You:

a. Write "Happy Birthday" and sign your name
b. Write a personal note and sign your name
c. Sign your name
d. Slip the card into the envelope and send it off

What's your favorite kind of test?

a. Short answer
b. Multiple choice
c. Essay
d. I don't like any tests!

Tally up your scores and take a look at your results!

Mostly A's? Try this: Write down bits and pieces of conversations with friends, journal with favorite quotations, or do a back-and-forth journaling exercise with a friend, where you write one thing and she writes the next thing. Be on the lookout for journaling inspiration everywhere you go (think billboards, signs and magazine advertisements).

Mostly B's? Try this: Journal in lists or make up your own fun journaling code! Use stickers and scrapbooking embellishments. Write fill-in-the-blank journaling. Journal with just an assortment of randomly selected words that describe a favorite photograph or something you love.

Mostly C's? Try this: Journal like you're telling a story to a friend. Or think about journaling as a creative writing exercise. Your journaling is probably already pretty interesting to read—keep challenging yourself to make it real and keep it as fun as possible!

Mostly D's? Try this: Create your own journaling shorthand! Use your favorite abbreviations as often as you'd like. Think about making a little guide to these sayings that you can put in the front of your scrapbook (our grandkids, for example, might not know that LOL means laughing out loud!).

challenge #27

Scrapbook Those Silly Photos

I know you have them. Well, at least just one. You know what I'm talking about—a silly photo. My dad always makes faces when I take his picture, so I finally decided to put one on a page. If you don't have a silly photograph to scrapbook, go and take one. You might be surprised at just how much fun it can be!

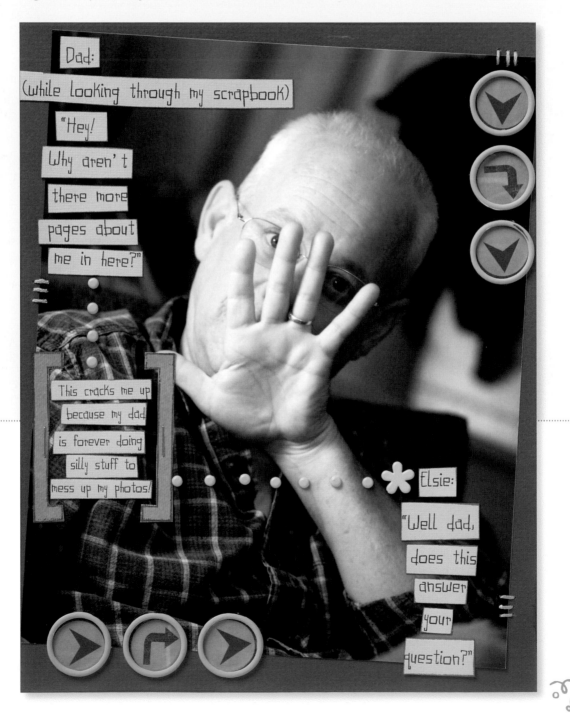

RIBBONS & bows

august 05

ALEXA
"Mom, Can I do your hair?"

MOM
"Sure. What is it going to look like?"

ALEXA
"It's a surprise. You'll see"

MOM
"Wow! That's a lot of bows!"

ALEXA
"Mom, You can *never* have enough ribbons and bows!"

QUESTION (on opposite page) by Elsie Flannigan
SUPPLIES Textured cardstock: Bazzill Basics Paper; Patterned paper: Autumn Leaves: Rubber stamp: Fontwerks; Brads· Doodlebug Design and Making Memories; Metal frames: Scrapworks; Computer font: 2Peas Betty Robot, downloaded from www.twopeasinabucket.com; Other: Staples and thread.

RIBBONS & BOWS by Julia Scattaregia
SUPPLIES Patterned papers: Fontwerks; Round ribbon charms, bubble letters and rub-ons: Li'l Davis Designs; Ribbon: Li'l Davis Designs, Making Memories and C.M. Offray & Son; Painted gridworks: Creative Imaginations; Stamping ink: StazOn, Tsukineko; Label tape: Dymo.

FUN MOM by Danielle Donaldson
SUPPLIES Patterned papers: Chatterbox; Rubber stamps and rub-ons: Making Memories; Pens: EK Success, Stampin' Up! and American Crafts; Stamping ink: Stampin' Up!; Punch: QuicKutz; Watercolor crayons: Stampin' Up!; Epoxy accents: Provo Craft; Ribbon: American Crafts.

I want to think of my kids as someone who can be just as silly as they are. I want them to remember me as the

FUN mom

LAUREN-MOM-CLAY

challenge #28

Document a Day in Your Life

How do you spend a typical day? I know, you might think your life is just the same old thing all the time. But your children and grandchildren will be fascinated to know the details that make up your daily routine. Believe me, it's worth it to create a page that chronicles a day in your life. You're worth it!

SomeTimes my life is...

1 two weeks worth of dirty laundry

2 being a taxi service for my kids

3 a sink full of dirty dishes that no one seems to notice but me

And SOmEtImes my life is...

1 eating dinner on the back porch as the sun sets

2 sweet little notes in envelopes from my kids

3 a never-ending supply of fresh antique roses

Life happens. But when it's good, it's very VERY GOOD

LIFE HAPPENS (on opposite page) by Mellette Berezoski

SUPPLIES Textured cardstock, rub-on letters, number stickers, fabric flowers, ribbon, gem brad and stick pin: Making Memories; Patterned papers: KI Memories, Making Memories, BasicGrey, Chatterbox and Anna Griffin; Round letter tab: Autumn Leaves; Cardstock tags: KI Memories; Metal house charm: Creative Imaginations; Computer fonts: 2Peas International and 2Peas Organic, downloaded from www.twopeasinabucket.com.

PIECES OF ME by Vicki Harvey

SUPPLIES Patterned papers: Scenic Route Paper Co. and Mustard Moon; Chipboard letters: BasicGrey; Letter stickers: Doodlebug Design; Chipboard flowers and acrylic paint: Making Memories; Rickrack: Jo-Ann Stores; Computer font: CB Wednesday, "Journaling Genie" CD, Chatterbox.

elsie's box

For an easy way to document a day in your life, just make a photocopy of your day planner or of a grocery list or to-do list. I know you might think it would look messy—but think about how cool it would be if your kids discovered it one day. And, you can also make a little hidden journaling slot for it, too!

challenge #29

Journal an Unexpected Turn

Life is full of interesting twists and turns. If you've ever had a dream and then been surprised at how your life really turned out, you'll know what I mean. For this challenge, take a look at an event or a time in your life when you thought things might be a certain way but ended up completely different!

it's not easy BEING GREEN

In the movies, pregnant women always glow. They radiate light and happiness and maternal warmth. Me? I radiated all right. Like a nuclear power plant. For the first five months of my pregnancy, I was neon green. Morning sickness is somewhat of a misnomer, since my morning sickness started at midnight and lasted until 11:59. Luckily, the men at work gave me a wide birth. Two hours late? Ate saltines all day? Fine. We just don't want to know the details. The best news of all? When my nausea disappeared in my sixth month, the bad memories did, too. And I can't help but think how worth it the nausea was. Nic thinks it's nutty, but in retrospect, all that bathroom time means nothing. It's all worth it, and I haven't even seen that precious baby boy yet. I'd do it again—even with the green. 12/05

My name is Vicki and I am a stay at home mom. If you would have told me 20 years ago that I would be uttering those words, I'd have laughed in your face. You see, I was going to be a doctor - a pediatric cardiologist to be exact. I had my life planned out and I was driven. So, off to college I went and boy were my eyes opened quickly. The biggest lesson I learned was that the world is not black and white and some plans do not work out like you think they will. It's amazing how life keeps throwing you curve balls until you get to where you are supposed to be - signs from God maybe? Or just His master plan? Through some extensive soul searching, I've recently felt a great comfort about where I am in my life. I've realized that God had a greater plan for me than I had for myself. I am supposed to be a mother. I am passionate about it. I've been given the priviledge of raising three souls. I love being home when my kids get off the bus. I love that they know I am here for them. Volunteering at school in their classrooms fills me up like nothing I've ever done. I feel so happy after I've done that. I know that they will grow up and my job will then be to let them go. I also know that will be very hard, but I will trust that God has the next part of His plan in place for me. I'll be excited to see what unexpected path my life will take then.

THE WEDDING PLANNER (on opposite page)
by Elsie Flannigan
SUPPLIES Textured cardstock: Bazzill Basics Paper; Patterned paper, stickers and tags: KI Memories; Twill tape: 7gypsies; Acrylic paint: Making Memories; Other: Ribbon, buttons and thread.

IT'S NOT EASY BEING GREEN by Traci Turchin
SUPPLIES Patterned paper: Scrapworks; Computer font: Univers, downloaded from the Internet; Software: Adobe Photoshop CS, Adobe Systems.

MY UNEXPECTED LIFE by Vicki Harvey
SUPPLIES Patterned papers: Making Memories, Chatterbox and Mustard Moon; String envelope: Paper Depot; Photo corners: Canson; Rub-on letters: Chatterbox; Letter stickers: Sonnets, Creative Imaginations; Chipboard letters, label holder and index tab: Heidi Swapp for Advantus; Rub-on date, flower, lace and button: Making Memories; Brads: Creative Impressions; "Mother's Day" rub-on: Autumn Leaves; Transparency: Office Depot; Computer font: Times New Roman, Microsoft Word.

Digitally Alter a Photograph

I love taking photographs and challenging myself by doing cool things with my photo software. I'd like to challenge you to do the same. Look how Traci changed the colors of a photo (such a romantic background on the cover of her "Love" mini album) and digitally sliced and stretched the photos on her "Party" layout. You could also take a cue from Rachel and experiment by giving a photo an artistic effect. Whatever you choose, your challenge here is to digitally alter a photo in such a way that it helps enhance the story on your layout.

LOVE by Traci Turchin
SUPPLIES Software: Adobe Photoshop CS, Adobe Systems; Computer font: Baskerville, downloaded from the Internet. Cover photo by Larry Rice Photography.

I got to meet Emily, the newest edition to the Cooper family.

There's nothing quite as good as a family gathering to celebrate a birthday. Cupcakes, cousins, and laughs. May 2005

P A R T Y

JJ has such an easy-going personality that the "Life is Good" hat could not have a better model!

Nic and JJ set up and played with my old Lego trainset. I'm almost entirely sure that I know who enjoyed it the most!

PARTY by Traci Turchin
SUPPLIES Software: Adobe Photoshop CS, Adobe Systems; Computer font: Univers, downloaded from the Internet.

A LITTLE WISER by Rachel Ludwig
SUPPLIES Textured cardstock: Bazzill Basics Paper; Ribbon: Scrapworks; Rub-ons: Making Memories, Scrapworks, Fontwerks and Autumn Leaves; Digital brush: Rhonna Farrer, www.twopeasinabucket.com; Computer font: AL Worn Machine, "15 Typewriter Fonts" CD, Autumn Leaves.

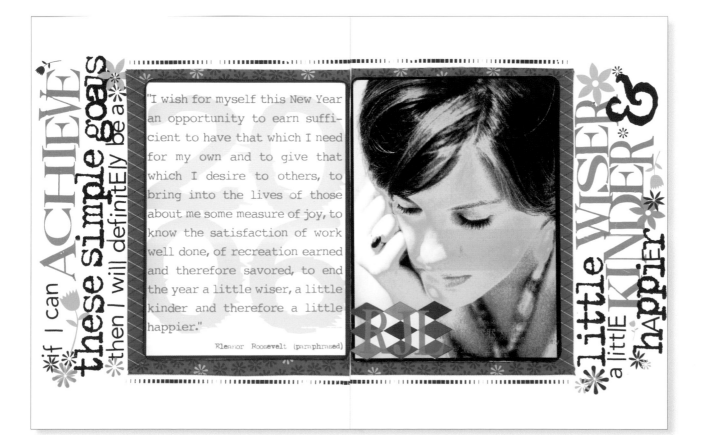

if I can ACHIEVE these simple goals then I will definitEly be a

"I wish for myself this New Year an opportunity to earn sufficient to have that which I need for my own and to give that which I desire to others, to bring into the lives of those about me some measure of joy, to know the satisfaction of work well done, of recreation earned and therefore savored, to end the year a little wiser, a little kinder and therefore a little happier."

Eleanor Roosevelt (paraphrased)

little WISER a littlE KINDER & happier

challenge #31

Celebrate a Great Person

We all have special people in our lives—people who have made a difference. I think it's so important to create scrapbook pages that help share the essence of who they are and what they mean to us. For this challenge, create a layout that celebrates a special someone in your life!

WONDERFUL (on opposite page) by Elsie Flannigan
SUPPLIES Textured cardstock: Making Memories; Patterned papers:
Making Memories, Anna Griffin and KI Memories; Rub-ons: KI
Memories; Flowers: Prima; Other: Buttons and thread.

FRANCIS GREGORY by Traci Turchin
SUPPLIES Patterned papers: KI Memories; Chatterbox; foof-a-La,
Autumn Leaves; Wild Asparagus, My Mind's Eye; Brad: Making
Memories; Stickers and pen: American Crafts; Clip: Rob and Bob
Studio, Provo Craft; Other: Folder and photo turn.

A GROOVY KIND OF LOVE by Vicki Harvey
SUPPLIES Patterned papers: All My Memories, Making Memories
and Scenic Route Paper Co.; Letter stickers and rub-ons: Chatterbox;
Punches: EK Success; Pen: Pigment Pro, American Crafts; Pop-up adhesive dots: Zots, Therm O Web; Acrylic paint: Making Memories; Rubber
stamp: Office Depot; Stamping ink: Stampin' Up!; Computer font:
Teletype, downloaded from the Internet.

Play with Photo Proportions

Have a photograph you just love? Here's the challenge: feature your photograph predominantly on your layout by making it a large portion of your background. Here, Traci and I show two examples of how you can cover about two-thirds of your background with a photo. Try this technique digitally or with a traditionally printed photo.

I'm in my sixth month of pregnancy and finally seeing the light. The morning sickness finally stopped, this baby's kicks cannot be ignored, and my profile is decidely pregnant. My cheeks are rounder, my waist is a thing of the past, my body is a roadmap of veins and burst capillaries, and yet somehow I've never felt more beautiful. A big part of that is Nic, who never misses an opportunity to pat my belly or tell me how cute I look. It's made this period one of the happiest of my life. To carry this visible reminder of our growing family is nothing short of a miracle.

GLOW

GLOW by Traci Turchin

SUPPLIES Photo-editing software: Adobe Photoshop, Adobe Systems; Computer font: Baskerville, downloaded from www.linotype.com.

Photo caption within image:
There are only 3 colors, 10 digits, and 7 notes; it's what we do with them that's important. —Jim Rohn

Journaling within image:
DOREN is such A talented MusiciAN He is mostLY into Guitar right Now. His FAVORITE BANDS are GreenDAY + Weezer

DOREN by Elsie Flannigan

SUPPLIES Textured cardstock: Bazzill Basics Papers; Patterned paper, quote sticker and tag: KI Memories; Acrylic paint: Making Memories and Heidi Swapp for Advantus; Brads: American Crafts and Doodlebug Design; Other: Buttons and fabric paint.

elsie's box

Try playing with other photo proportions as well. Perhaps you want your photo to make up half of your page, and your journaling and embellishments to make up the other half. Or, what if your photo was one-fourth of your page and your journaling and embellishments were the other three-fourths? Have fun! Make it work for you!

challenge #33

Document Yourself

Who's the most important person you may be forgetting to scrapbook? Well, it could be you. Are you in your scrapbooks? Will future generations look through your albums and understand who you are today? My challenge to you is to scrapbook yourself at this moment in your life.

To relieve stress, I clean the house. I love to clean, it's very therapeutic for me.

I have a fear of heights and a fear of public speaking. I try to avoid both as much as possible.

I have always wanted to write a children's book.

Every year for my birthday, we celebrate by eating crawfish. Even my picky eater, Maysie, rolls up her sleeves and digs in. We can eat more than 12 pounds of those little mudbugs between the four of us.

Someday I hope to live in Sisters, Oregon. Hard to believe a place that breath-taking actually exists.

I would love to be Oprah for a day. It must be incredibly rewarding to be able to touch and change people's lives the way she does.

Words I live by: carpe diem, sister! You only get one chance at this life. Make every day count.

Mellette 9/2005

a little something about

TICKET TO RIDE (on opposite page)
by Maria Grace Abuzman

SUPPLIES Patterned papers: 7gypsies; Letter stamps: River City Rubber Works; Stamping ink: Tsukineko; Rub-ons: Making Memories; Dee's Designs, My Mind's Eye; Ribbon: Li'l Davis Designs; Labels: Chronicle Books; Computer font: AL Post Master, downloaded from www.twopeasinabucket.com.

A LITTLE SOMETHING ABOUT ME
by Mellette Berezoski

SUPPLIES Textured cardstock: Bazzill Basics Paper; Patterned papers: Chatterbox; Eyelets and trinket pin: Making Memories; Digital brushes: Chick Pea Kit by Rhonna Farrer, www.two-peasinabucket.com; Pearl charm: The Card Connection, Hirschberg Schutz & Co.; Computer font: Times New Roman, Microsoft Word; Other: Silk flower and ribbon.

IN LIVING COLOR by Danielle Thompson

SUPPLIES Textured cardstock and buttons: Bazzill Basics Paper; Patterned papers: Scrapworks and Scenic Route Paper Co.; Rub-on letters: KI Memories; Letter stickers: Autumn Leaves and BasicGrey; Fabric "C" sticker: Scrapworks; Epoxy letter stickers: MOD, Autumn Leaves; Mini brads: Making Memories; Rhinestones: Westrim Crafts; Embroidery floss: DMC; Pen: Uni-ball, Sanford; Other: Felt.

In COLOR

L i v i n g

challenge #34

Add Someone Else's Handwriting

Our handwriting gives such a great glimse into who we are as people. It's important to include our handwriting on our layouts, but I also think it's fun to integrate real and authentic notes from the people we love, too. I know that writing notes may seem like a lost art these days, but if you have a handwritten note from a child or a loved one, look for a way to include it on a page that celebrates that person. And don't be afraid to ask someone to write you a note or a list you can put on a layout, too!

100% BOY (on opposite page) by Kendra McCracken

SUPPLIES Textured cardstock: Bazzill Basics Paper, Colorbök and unknown; Patterned paper, photo anchors, loose-leaf rings, jump rings and long brads: Junkitz; Chipboard stars: Making Memories; Rub-ons and rubber stamps: Fontwerks; Label tape: Dymo; Ribbon: C.M. Offray & Son and unknown; Stamping ink: Stampabilities; Computer font: 8 Track, downloaded from www.dafont.com.

ARTIST by Vicki Harvey

SUPPLIES Patterned papers: Daisy D's Paper Co. and Paper Adventures; Ribbon: May Arts; Embroidery floss: DMC; Chipboard letter: BasicGrey; Letter stickers: American Crafts; Metal-rimmed tag and acrylic paint: Making Memories; Pen: Pigment Pro, American Crafts; Photo-corner punch: EK Success; Stitching template: Li'l Davis Designs; Computer font: Times New Roman, Microsoft Word; Other: Rickrack.

GOALS FOR 2006 by Elsie Flannigan
SUPPLIES Patterned papers: American Crafts and KI Memories; Photo corners: Heidi Swapp for Advantus; Acrylic accents: KI Memories; Brads: Mermaid Tears; Other: Buttons and thread.

challenge # 35

Make It Sparkle

I'll admit it. I love pretty things! And I love incorporating pretty things onto my pages. Sparkly, shiny rhinestones are just one of my favorite ways to add bling to my layouts. I think there's room for something sparkly on almost any page. For this challenge, add a bit of sparkle to your next page. Remember to choose something that fits the mood of your layout and helps express your personality. Use just a little or a lot—whatever best helps tell your story!

Creativity is inventing, experimenting, growing, taking risks, breaking rules, making mistakes, and having fun. —Mary Lou Cook

Rachel + Elsie. fall of '05

THIS GIRL (on opposite page) by Elsie Flannigan

SUPPLIES *Textured cardstock:* Die Cuts With a View; *Patterned papers:* Chatterbox; *Acrylic paint:* Making Memories; *Pen:* Uni-ball, Sanford; *Fabric:* Amy Butler; *Rub-ons:* Dee's Designs, My Mind's Eye; *Other:* Buttons and ribbon.

CREATIVITY IS by Elsie Flannigan

SUPPLIES *Textured cardstock:* Bazzill Basics Paper; *Patterned papers:* KI Memories; Sassafras Lass; Anna Griffin; Chloe's Closet, Imagination Project; *Rubber stamp:* Hero Arts; *Stamping ink:* ColorBox, Clearsnap; *Quote sticker:* KI Memories; *Ribbon:* Doodlebug Design and C.M. Offray & Son; *Epoxy accents and bezel brad:* MOD, Autumn Leaves; *Brads:* American Crafts; *Other:* Sequins, buttons and fabric paint.

EXPOSED by Kendra McCracken

SUPPLIES *Textured cardstock:* Bazzill Basics Paper; *Patterned papers:* Daisy D's Paper Co. and Junkitz; *Clips and buttons:* Junkitz; *Brads, chipboard letters and rub-ons:* Making Memories; *Ribbon:* C.M. Offray & Son; *Rub-on borders:* Fontwerks; *Woven flourishes:* foof-a-La, Autumn Leaves; *Stamping ink:* StazOn, Tsukineko; *Computer font:* Immoral, downloaded from www.dafont.com; *Other:* Acrylic paint, transparency, sequins, rhinestones, flowers, lace, fiber and jewelry tag.

SHE'S EXPOSED BUT still FIRMLY ROOTED

Moments Like This

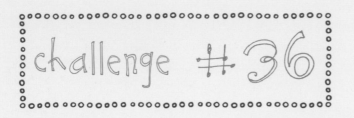

Scrapbook a Life-Long Love

Some memories and influences will stay with us forever. For example, I've literally been taking photographs forever and will always be a photographer. Vicki has loved Winnie the Pooh since she was a little girl (and even wanted a photograph of him as an adult on her family's latest visit to Disney World!). Snap photos and show off a life-long love on a layout!

I'm not sure who was more thrilled about seeing Winnie the Pooh - me or the kids. You see, I've been the world's biggest Pooh fan since I was about 7 years old and Santa brought me my very own Pooh bear. I couldn't sleep without him until I was in sixth grade and he still holds a very dear place in my heart.

When we went to Disney World this summer, Sandi was kind enough to get us reservations at the Pooh character lunch. I was so excited! I couldn't even eat my lunch until I had my photo taken with my beloved Pooh bear.

June '05

POOH (on opposite page) by Vicki Harvey

SUPPLIES Patterned papers: Chatterbox, Paper Adventures, Sandylion, Lasting Impressions for Paper and Hot Off The Press; Chipboard letters: Heidi Swapp for Advantus; Flower punch: EK Success; Embroidery floss: DMC; Decorative-edge scissors: Fiskars; Computer font: Americana, Microsoft Word; Other: Vintage buttons and staples.

LIFE-LONG LOVE by Elsie Flannigan

SUPPLIES Textured cardstock: Bazzill Basics Paper; Patterned papers: Christina Cole for Provo Craft, KI Memories and Scrapworks; Decorative tape: Heidi Swapp for Advantus; Ribbon: C.M. Offray & Son; Other: Fabric paint and staples.

elsie's box

Those things we hold dear forever deserve a place in our scrapbooks because they say so much about who we are. Another approach? Choose a personality trait you've had since childhood (stubbornness, happiness, determination, creativity) and trace it through your life on a scrapbook page.

challenge #37

Make It Edgy

Decorative-edged scissors are one of my favorite classic scrapbooking supplies. I love adding a pinking or a scalloped edge to just a small portion of my layout. My advice? A little bit of a pretty edge goes a long way, so use this tool with care—but do use it!

bloonies

LOVE (on opposite page) by Elsie Flannigan
SUPPLIES Textured cardstock: Bazzill Basics Paper; Patterned papers: KI Memories and Autumn Leaves; Stickers: KI Memories and Li'l Davis Designs; Rub-ons: KI Memories; Other: Fabric paint, rhinestones and ribbon.

B'LOONIES by Mellette Berezoski
SUPPLIES Patterned papers: Karen Foster Design, Scenic Route Paper Co. and BasicGrey; Ribbon: Making Memories and Autumn Leaves; Foam stamp, acrylic paint, rub-on letters and mini brads: Making Memories; Button: Autumn Leaves; Acrylic accent: KI Memories; Metal washers: Nostalgiques, EK Success; Tab: 3M; Pen: Zig Photo Signature, EK Success; Decorative-edge scissors: Fiskars.

DESTINATION HONEYMOON by Maria Grace Abuzman
SUPPLIES Patterned papers: Scenic Route Paper Co. and Making Memories; Rub-ons: Fontwerks and Heidi Swapp for Advantus; Ribbon: Maya Road; Flower: Making Memories.

challenge #38

Start with a Number

Need a fun way to start a page? It's easy—start with a number. Make a top-10 list. Or, look for number-themed accents to build your page around. Numbers are everywhere! Build a page around a telephone number, a shoe size, an age, a year, a "good luck" number or more!

10 THINGS I LOVE by Elsie Flannigan

SUPPLIES Textured cardstock: Bazzill Basics Paper; Patterned papers: BasicGrey and Scenic Route Paper Co.; Chipboard letters and photo corners: Heidi Swapp for Advantus; Brads: Magic Scraps and Making Memories; Other: Buttons, pen and thread.

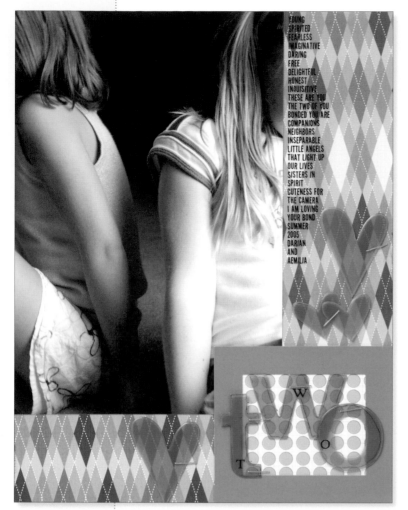

YOUNG
SPIRITED
FEARLESS
IMAGINATIVE
DARING
FREE
DELIGHTFUL
HONEST
INQUISITIVE
THESE ARE YOU
THE TWO OF YOU
BONDED YOU ARE
COMPANIONS
NEIGHBORS
INSEPARABLE
LITTLE ANGELS
THAT LIGHT UP
OUR LIVES
SISTERS IN
SPIRIT
CUTENESS FOR
THE CAMERA
I AM LOVING
YOUR BOND
SUMMER
2005
DARIAN
AND
AEMILIA

TWO by Joy Bohon

SUPPLIES Patterned papers: Chatterbox; Transparency: Hammermill; Metal frame: Making Memories; Acetate hearts and letters: Heidi Swapp for Advantus; Stamping ink: All Night Media; Rub-on letters: 7gypsies; Computer font: Tasklist, downloaded from www.twopeasinabucket.com; Other: Staples.

GIRLY SHOES by Julie Scattaregia

SUPPLIES Textured cardstock: Bazzill Basics Paper; Patterned paper and large photo turn: 7gypsies; Embellished background, wooden numbers, rub-ons and ribbon: Li'l Davis Designs; Negative strip: Narratives, Creative Imaginations; Leaf clip: Scrapworks; Metal corner frame: Embellish It!; Small photo turn and rub-ons: Making Memories; Label tape: Dymo.

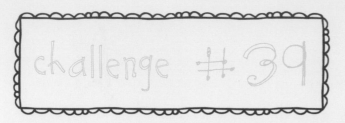

Go Mega!

It's fun to do something unexpected on a layout—like surprise your readers with a title spelled out with mega-sized letters! It doesn't matter if you choose acetate letters, die-cut letters, stencil letters or hand-cut letters. It's not always polite to shout in public, but sometimes you just need to get the message across on your page. So, go mega!

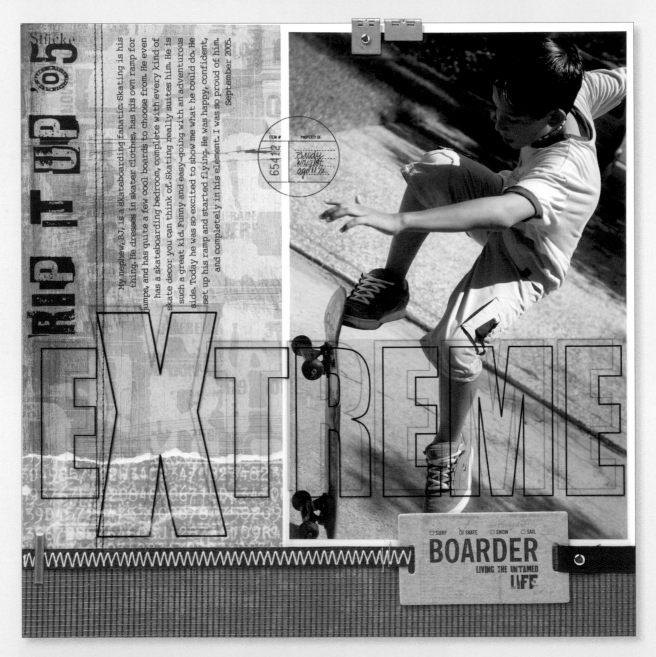

EXTREME (on opposite page) by Mellette Berezoski
SUPPLIES Patterned papers: BasicGrey; Art Warehouse, Creative Imaginations; Daisy D's Paper Co.; Mesh: Magic Mesh; Tag, hinges, brads and decorative rub-on: Making Memories; Letter stickers: Art Warehouse, Creative Imaginations; Stitched leather border: Li'l Davis Designs; Brad bar: Karen Foster Design; Transparency: 3M; Computer fonts: AL Postmaster, downloaded from www.twopeasinabucket.com; Impact, downloaded from www.dafont.com.

WE PRAY by Elsie Flannigan
SUPPLIES Textured cardstock: Bazzill Basics Paper and Prism Papers; Patterned papers: Autumn Leaves, KI Memories, K&Company, Scenic Route Paper Co. and Chatterbox; Brads: Doodlebug Design; Ribbon: Li'l Davis Designs and Lasting Impressions for Paper; Stickers: Li'l Davis Designs.

BEAUTIFUL by Rachel Ludwig
SUPPLIES Textured cardstock: Bazzill Basics Paper; Rub-ons: Scrapworks; Letter stickers: Gin-X, Imagination Project; Computer font: Myriad, downloaded from the Internet.

challenge #40

Use Supplies Unexpectedly

You've probably got tons of extra supplies that you sometimes wonder how to use. My answer? I challenge myself to use my supplies in unexpected ways. It stretches my creativity and makes my pages totally unique. Challenge yourself to create a circle with a line or stickers, or design an arrow from a photo corner and a piece of ribbon, or add jewels to your hair (right on the photo).

FAMILY by Elsie Flannigan

SUPPLIES Patterned paper and ribbon: KI Memories; Acrylic paint and velvet stickers: Making Memories; Epoxy stickers: Autumn Leaves; Photo corners: Heidi Swapp for Advantus; Other: Buttons and thread.

el Love this photo
of t.j. and cocoa Napping
together ♥ this is the
Kind of sweet Moment I
used to DReaM About. so
peaceful-so cute- so
cozy. is our life ALWays
Like this? Heck No. But this
is a moment in our journey
that I want to remember ★

sleeping soundly **HERE** **COMFORT** **HAPPY** home **support**

LOVE Welcome HOME
Warmth getting cozy in our New Home Photo TAKEN... 2007
ADORE home family

NAP by Elsie Flannigan
SUPPLIES Textured cardstock: Bazzill Basics Paper; Patterned paper: KI Memories; Stickers and acrylic paint: Making Memories; Other: Buttons and flower.

A LITTLE BIRDIE TOLD ME by Elsie Flannigan
SUPPLIES Patterned papers: BasicGrey; My Mind's Eye; Sassafras Lass; Chloe's Closet, Imagination Project; Quote sticker: KI Memories; Rubber stamps: Hero Arts; Acrylic paint: Making Memories; Other: Rhinestones.

A little birdie told me...

Art is the only way to run away without leaving home. —Twyla Tharp

challenge #41

Scrapbook a Major Accomplishment

I know, it's sometimes hard to stop and scrapbook about yourself and your goals and dreams and what you've accomplished in life. But it's important. It's good for you to see where you've been and what you've accomplished—and besides that, future generations will be proud to see that you broke a board in Tae Kwon Do (like Julie) or made your own rules about what to wear (like Joy)!

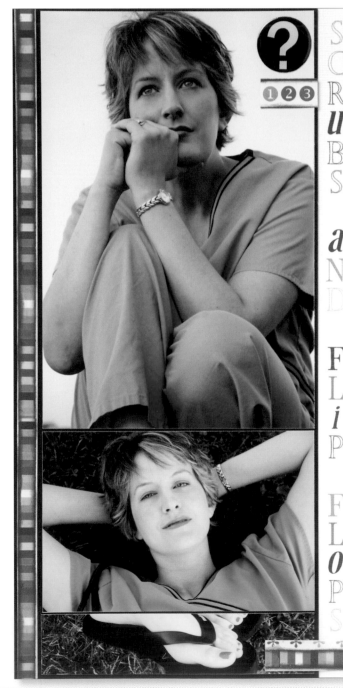

Scrubs and flip flops

Probably not the outfit you expect to find your doctor wearing in small town America, at least not in this neck of the woods, but especially this summer, that has become my outfit of choice at work. I have lots of excuses. Scrubs are utilitarian, functional, they allow me easy entry from the delivery ward to my office, they are comfortable, they mix and match seamlessly, they mark my profession. But. As I slip them on each morning I recall that old rule from residency-that we weren't to wear scrubs to the office, that we should "dress up", that even post-call we weren't allowed to slip by in the old scrubs. That twang of guilt, I recall it, then I smile, for here I am, after 11 long years of training, my own boss, governed by my own rules, having earned my own freedom- I can make new rules. And so it is. Scrubs and flip flops.

But bosses and old residency rules aren't the only ones in this equation, for we can't forget the other very important part of my practice-my patients. Surveys have been done, on how patients prefer their physicians to dress, and overwhelmingly they desire them to dress professionally, to be well kempt, to look the part. I know this and I just smile, for honestly I give each day to try to know these people beneath their surface, and I believe that they do the same for me. My dress, and my demeaner, it is approachable, it is real.. I am like any other soul on this street. My scrub claid shoulder is more appropriate for tears than would be a well pressed white shirt, my painted toenails clad in flip flops make me more like my patients that I care for than would a 2 inch pump. I am approachable, I am real. I am a harried working mother who slips on scrubs in the morning as she runs out the door, slipping into flip flops just because. This is me.. scrubs and flip flops and all. Told you I had lots of excuses.

TAKE TIME TO PLAY

2005

I am not invincible, but I am **strong**.

I am not fearless, but I am **courageous**.

I am not young, but I am **youthful**.

Carmel Te
To Julie wondo.
Happy Birthday?
생일축하합니
2005. 9. 21

FIRST TIME BREAKING A BOARD

SCRUBS AND FLIP-FLOPS (on opposite page) by Joy Bohon
SUPPLIES Patterned paper and epoxy sticker: Christina Cole for Provo Craft; Computer fonts: 2Peas Wynngate, downloaded from www.twopeasinabucket.com; Casablanca Antique, downloaded from the Internet.

TAE KWON DO by Julie Scattaregia
SUPPLIES Patterned paper, library card and metal frames: Daisy D's Paper Co.; Metal letters, foam stamps, brads and ribbon: Making Memories; Arrow tab and negative strip: Creative Imaginations; Pin: Nostalgiques, EK Success; Bubble letters: Li'l Davis Designs; Acrylic paint: Delta Technical Coatings.

elsie's box

{ It's also good to scrapbook the little accomplishments in life—it'll help you see that you are making progress toward a goal! Maybe you meditate for five minutes a day, or maybe you're taking baby steps on a project that's really important to you. No matter how small the achievement, it's worthy of your scrapbook! }

challenge #42

Create a Stylish Photo Frame

Who says all the pretty photo frames can't be on your scrapbook pages? I love creating my own photo frames with bits and pieces of the supplies I love the most! This is a great way to add your own personal style to a page while using up leftover scraps of patterned paper and ribbon. Have fun with it!

PLAY (on opposite page) by Elsie Flannigan

SUPPLIES Textured cardstock: Bazzill Basics Paper; Stickers: Li'l Davis Designs; Epoxy accents: Autumn Leaves; Rub-ons: Fontwerks, KI Memories, Autumn Leaves and K&Company.

SENIOR PROM by Elsie Flannigan

SUPPLIES Textured cardstock: Bazzill Basics Paper; Patterned papers: KI Memories, Chatterbox, Christina Cole for Provo Craft, Scrapworks and Anna Griffin; Acetate accents: Heidi Swapp for Advantus; Tag: KI Memories; Acrylic paint: Making Memories.

THERE ARE TIMES by Elsie Flannigan

SUPPLIES Textured cardstock: Bazzill Basics Paper; Mask, foam stamps and acrylic paint: Heidi Swapp for Advantus; Stickers: American Crafts; Flowers: Prima; Pen: Uni-ball, Sanford; Tabs: Autumn Leaves.

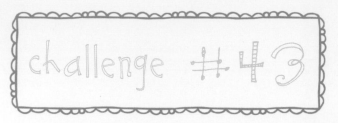

challenge #43

Scrapbook Your Favorite Food

What foods do you crave? What foods fit your different moods? Is there a food you just discovered and can't get enough of? The foods we love tell so much about who we are. I think it's really fun to take a moment and scrapbook a favorite food or snack. I encourage you to create pages that share the little things in your life right now (I think it'll be fun for my children to peek into my life as a young married woman!).

SNACK LOVE (on opposite page) by Maria Grace Abuzman

SUPPLIES Patterned papers: Scenic Route Paper Co.; Stickers: Li'l Davis Designs and 7gypsies; Rub-ons: Fontwerks and Heidi Swapp for Advantus; Ribbon: May Arts.

SUSHI LOVE by Elsie Flannigan

SUPPLIES Patterned papers: BasicGrey and Autumn Leaves; Stickers: American Crafts; Chipboard word: Heidi Swapp for Advantus; Label: Li'l Davis Designs; Rubber stamp: Hero Arts; Stamping ink: ColorBox, Clearsnap; Acrylic paint and adhesive jewels: Making Memories; Ribbon: C.M. Offray & Son; Other: Bamboo.

elsie's box

{ On the flip side, scrapbook your least favorite food! Why don't you like it? Do you think you'll ever eat it again? What do people think when you refuse to eat it? Have you disliked it forever? }

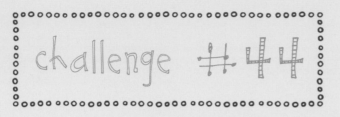

Create a Fun Photo Mat

Mellette has taken photo mats to a new level! Just look at how the strips of patterned paper under her photographs draw your eye right to the shots. Mellette says, "On the page about my children, I used various patterned papers to signify the five different children in the photo." I challenge you to take this idea and experiment with it on your own pages!

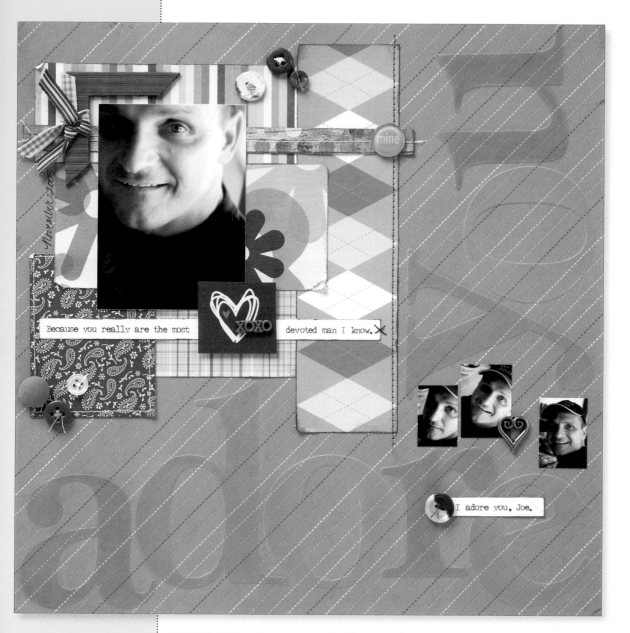

Because you really are the most XOXO devoted man I know.

mine

I adore you, Joe.

THE FABULOUS FIVE (on opposite page) by Mellette Berezoski

SUPPLIES Textured cardstock: Making Memories; Patterned papers: Karen Foster Design, Making Memories, 7gypsies and Chatterbox; Chipboard number, acrylic paint, letter stickers, leather photo corner, brads and gem sticker: Making Memories; Decorative tape: Heidi Swapp for Advantus; Rub-ons: 7gypsies; Label sticker: Avery; Computer fonts: 2Peas Weathered Fence and 2Peas Open Spaces, downloaded from www.twopeasinabucket.com; Mariette and Distress, downloaded from www.dafont.com.

I ADORE YOU, JOE by Mellette Berezoski

SUPPLIES Patterned papers: KI Memories, Chatterbox and Making Memories; Leather corner and metal charms: Making Memories; Monogram letters: BasicGrey; Ribbon and acrylic accent: KI Memories; Chalk: Craft-T Products; Stamping ink: Ranger Industries; Computer font: GF Halda, package unknown; Other: Buttons.

elsie's box

Here's something so fun to try: Go to the scrapbook store and look at the papers. Pull out five that represent your personality. Why did you pick those papers? What do they say about you? Do the papers work together or do they represent completely different parts of your personality? Now, I challenge you to make a fun photo mat for an "all about me" page using your selected papers!

challenge #45

Add an Arrow

I love the arrow as a design element. It's such an easy way to direct your reader's eye exactly where you want it to go. And the really fun thing about an arrow is that you can make it out of so many different things, including your leftover scraps of patterned paper, ribbons, photo corners, chipboard, triangle-shaped embellishments, stitching, floss, rickrack and more. Or even make it digital! Go ahead and add an arrow to your next layout!

LOVE LOOKS LIKE by Elsie Flannigan

SUPPLIES Textured cardstock: Bazzill Basics Paper; Patterned papers: Scenic Route Paper Co.; Ribbon: American Crafts and C.M. Offray & Son; Photo corner: Heidi Swapp for Advantus; Pen: Uni-ball, Sanford; Flowers: Prima; Other: Buttons and thread.

I don't know anyone that likes moving, and I'm no different. You'd think I'd be good at it by now. The move from England to the Thomsons', and then to the rental house, and then to the house in Issaquah, the moves we had to make at the end of each quarter while I lived at Alpha Delta Pi, and then moving my things home at the end of every year when I lived in the dorms. But I'm terrible at it. Nic's really not much better. He'll throw things away, just because he doesn't really want to pack them. I've watched him throw away packs of AA batteries, which everyone knows are like gold. When I moved to Virginia, I took all the "essentials" with me in the car. I lived with them, and them alone, for two months, so when all of my *stuff* showed up, I was left thinking "look at all this crap I have that I don't even need!" There were millions of books, of course, and tons of kitchen supplies I'd hoarded with my William Sonoma discount (supplies that became increasingly ironic as they gathered dust). A box or two of old and leaking toiletries and lots of lipstick...old magazines and out of season clothes. It turned out I didn't need any of "my things." Virginia was already home, just because Nic was there.

moving

MOVING by Traci Turchin

SUPPLIES Photo-editing software: Adobe Photoshop, Adobe Systems; Computer font: Univers, downloaded from www.linotype.com.

PARTNERS IN CRIME by Kendra McCracken

SUPPLIES Textured cardstock: Bazzill Basics Paper; Patterned papers: BasicGrey; Chipboard letters: Heidi Swapp for Advantus; Buttons: Bazzill Basics Paper, Chatterbox and Junkitz; Leather photo frame: Making Memories; Ribbon: C.M. Offray & Son; Border sticker: Close To My Heart; Embroidery floss: DMC; Computer font: Calvin and Hobbes, downloaded from www.dafont.com; Other: Beads, playing card and rickrack.

PARTNERS

iN cRIME

challenge #46

Play with Paint

Acrylic paint—it's not just for backgrounds anymore! I think acrylic paint is one of the most versatile supplies out there. For one, it comes in hundreds of beautiful colors. And, you can use just a little on your layouts to create impact. On these pages, we used acrylic paint to make lines for journaling, stamped with it on a transparency to make a custom accent, and hand-painted journaling right on top of a photograph (make an extra print just in case you make a mistake). My challenge to you? Play with acrylic paint and find a way to use it within your own personal style.

ALIVE by Elsie Flannigan
SUPPLIES Patterned papers: KI Memories; Acrylic paint: Making Memories; Other: Sequins.

Catching bubbles in the shadows of our back porch-simply magical. 2005

BUBBLES by Joy Bohon
SUPPLIES Transparency: Hammermill; Epoxy letters: MOD, Autumn Leaves; Acrylic paint: Making Memories; Foam stamp: Heidi Swapp for Advantus; Brad: American Crafts; Computer font: SquareSerif, downloaded from the Internet.

SOLITUDE by Elsie Flannigan
SUPPLIES Patterned paper and cardstock flower: Elsie's own designs; Ribbon: May Arts, C.M. Offray & Son and Elsie's own design; Rub-ons and mailbox letter: Making Memories; Chipboard flower: Heidi Swapp for Advantus; Other: Buttons.

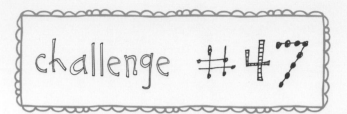

challenge #47

Find Inspiration: Home Decor

Guess what? Home decor is one of my favorite places to find inspiration for my scrapbook pages. Why? Well, if I love it in my home, I'll probably love it on my scrapbook pages, too. And some of the very best designers out there work in the home-decor industry, creating products to make our homes beautiful, warm and cozy. If you feel your home is a reflection of who you are, then I bet you'll find inspiration in home decor for your layouts, too!

I am beginning to understand that part of my job as your mother, as difficult as it may be, is to give you **wings.**

Aim for the stars, baby. Aim for the stars.

WINGS

WINGS (on opposite page) by Mellette Berezoski
SUPPLIES Patterned papers: Chatterbox and 7gypsies; Foam stamp, acrylic paint and chipboard letters: Making Memories; Transparency: Hammermill; Ribbon: May Arts; Beads: Magic Scraps; Embroidery floss: DMC; Computer font: James Fajardo, downloaded from www.dafont.com; Other: Vintage buttons.

OUR PRINCESS by Julie Scattaregia
SUPPLIES Patterned paper and rub-ons: Daisy D's Paper Co.; Metal word, clay letters and bubble word: Li'l Davis Designs; Metal screen, metal frame and metal ampersand: Making Memories; Negative strip: Narratives, Creative Imaginations; Stamping ink: Iridescent Ink, Dr. Ph. Martin's; Acrylic paint: Delta Technical Coatings; Ribbon: C.M. Offray & Son; Other: Silk flower and chenille fabric.

challenge #48

Find Inspiration: Fashion

I love fashion as scrapbook-page inspiration. I mean, think of the colors, the textures, the details you find in clothing and accessories. So many beautiful patterns and wonderful color combinations already put together for you! So much just waiting for you to discover and translate to your scrapbook pages!

MaR.
Ket

APRIL · 2005

treasure

I absolutely
LOVE the
antique + craft
market at the
Inman Park Festival
every year. I love
the ECLECTIC mix of items & also
people. I love the history that comes
with old things and the charm of
handmade crafts. Atlanta is like
no other with its FESTIVALS. People
come out in droves at these things. They
make me feel ALIVE. I love
taking COOPER! to these things too.
He is so cute soaking all the noises,
colors + smells in. I hope he
appreciates antiques + wes don't the way
we do!

INMAN PARK
festival

TWO OF A KIND (on opposite page) by Elsie Flannigan

SUPPLIES Textured cardstock: Prism Papers; Patterned paper: Scenic
Route Paper Co.; Decorative tape: Heidi Swapp for Advantus; Ribbon:
American Crafts and Elsie's own design; Acrylic paint: Making
Memories; Other: Rhinestones and fabric.

MARKET by Danielle Thompson

SUPPLIES Textured cardstock: Bazzill Basics Paper; Pens: Zig
Writers, EK Success; Metallic pen: Uni-ball, Sanford; Buttons:
SEI and EK Success; Yarn: Lion Brand Yarn; Rub-ons:
Making Memories; Letter stamps: Ma Vinci's Reliquary;
Stamping ink: VersaColor, Tsukineko; Mini letter-block beads:
Michaels; Chalk: Craf-T Products; Jewels: Kandi Corp.; Jewel
setter: Kandi Kane, Kandi Corp; Other: Staples.

challenge #49

Make Your Own Photo Corners

Embellished photo corners are awesome. Sure, they help draw attention to your photographs, but they're also little "mini canvases" where you can be artistic and express your personal style. You can make your own photo corners in so many ways. Here's one that's quick and easy:

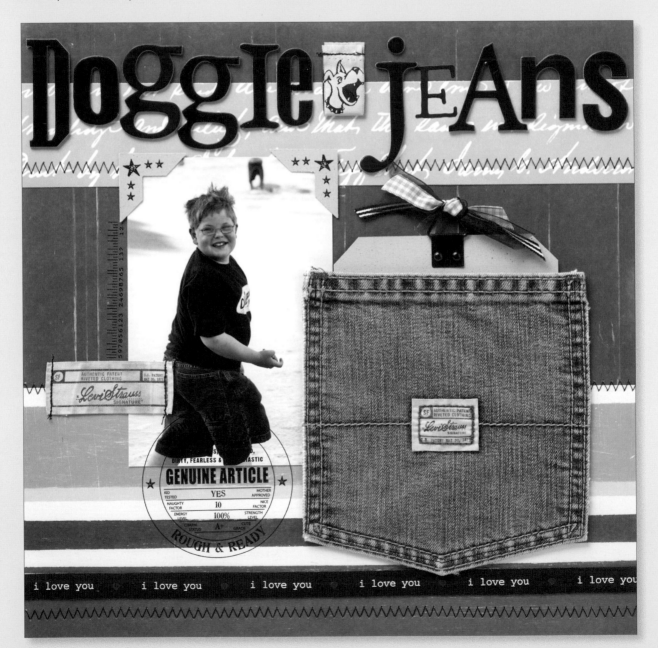

DOGGIE JEANS by Vicki Harvey

SUPPLIES Patterned papers: Rusty Pickle and Scenic Route Paper Co; Chipboard letters: Heidi Swapp for Advantus; "E" sticker: Doodlebug Design; Rub-on star and label: BasicGrey; Ribbon: Creative Impressions, Li'l Davis Designs, Stampin' Up!, Bobbin Ribbon and Morex; Picture hanger: Daisy D's Paper Co.; Photo-corner punch: EK Success; Computer font: CK Extra, "Fresh Fonts" CD, ; Other: Jeans pocket and tags, and thread.

Photo corner samples at right by Elsie Flannigan and Maria Grace Abuzman

step-by-step

Make Your Own Photo Corners

1. Sketch or trace the shape on patterned paper or cardstock.

2. Cut the shape out.

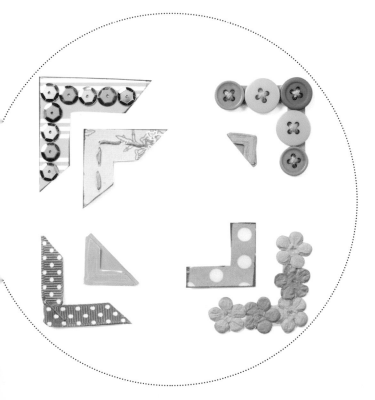

3. Add embellishments.

challenge #50

Just Tell a Great Story

Scrapbooking. It's about making a home for those fantastic stories that just beg to be told about your life. Whether it's a time when you surprised someone, a time when you set a trend or a time when you had a blast helping someone else, your stories deserve a place in your scrapbook. I know that we often start with the photo, but once in a while, just listen to the stories you find yourself telling your friends over and over again. Then ask yourself, "Hey, is that story in my scrapbook?" If not, now's a good time to give it a home!

Scott and i are beginning to get used to this ALONE TIME we have in our hands now that the kids have separate social lives. More often than not, we find ourselves running out of time & money to go out. The big discovery is that we don't have to go out to enjoy each others COMPANY!

It was about 7 or 8 at night and the doorbell rang. I answered it and found some neighborhood girls on a scavenger hunt. They rattled off a list of items they were in search of, one of which happened to be an Indigo Blue Crayon. Obviously, I'm quite the collector and told her to hang on a minute while I got one for her. I dumped a large rubbermaid bin in to a giant cardboard box to facilitate the search. By this time Scott came in to help. He asked me if I was sure there was such a thing. (Are you kidding me?) Alas, I could find two of every shade of blue, but not Indigo. I sent the girls on their way with some shade that I knew was similar.

Unreasonably frustrated and irritated, I continued my search in the big box. There had to be one Indigo Blue Crayon in the massive amount of crayons I had in front of me! Although not many would understand my need to find this crayon, Scott was right there with me. I consider my eye for color a badge of honor of sorts. When I finally found a single, Indigo Blue Crayon, I jumped up and down with excitment! Too bad the girls were long gone... or so I thought!

the STORY of the **indigo** *blue crayon*

Scott (who really could care less about crayons) pulled out his jeep and said, "Let's go find them!" We hopped in his jeep (in our pj's) and found them on the other side of our neighborhood. I jumped up and asked who still needed an Indigo Blue Crayon. The girls screamed and ran to the jeep, happily handed it to them!

Oh my gosh, how many men would do that?!

the
ugly
wreath

THE STORY OF THE INDIGO BLUE CRAYON
(on opposite page) by Danielle Donaldson

SUPPLIES Textured cardstock: Bo-Bunny Press; Patterned papers: Daisy D's Paper Co. and Chatterbox; Staples: Making Memories; Stamping ink and watercolor crayons: Stampin' Up!; Pens: EK Success, Stampin' Up! and American Crafts; Computer fonts: Indigo, downloaded from www.dafont.com; Prestige and Arial Bold, Microsoft Word; Pristina, package unknown.

THE UGLY WREATH by Traci Turchin

SUPPLIES Software: Adobe Photoshop CS, Adobe Systems; Patterned papers: KI Memories and BasicGrey; Acrylic accent: KI Memories; Ribbon: KI Memories and unknown; Brads: American Crafts; Computer font: Univers, downloaded from the Internet; Other: Staples.

DUCK TAPE by Elsie Flannigan

SUPPLIES Textured cardstock: Bazzill Basics Paper; Rub-ons, letters and ribbon: KI Memories.

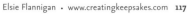

challenge #51

Fill a Background

There's just something I love about covering an entire background with handwriting, circles, buttons or other embellishments. It's a great way to add your personal style to a layout while creating a look that's warm and cozy all at the same time. Choose something you love and use it to fill in the entire background of your page!

This photo of me w/ BABY Trinity makes me so happy. It is SO weird for me to see my friends all having babies and even t.j's little brother! When we first got married I always assumed we would start our family pretty much right away... But Here We Are, 4 years later, still waiting. People used to warn us to wait a little while and enjoy marriage, now they worry that we aren't planning to have children. LOL! Well, no worries, we both want children very much, we are just waiting for the right time. Of course, we aren't really sure when that will be. I keep saying, "Not too soon, but not too long." Maybe just a year or two more? Nope ☺ Or 3? Is there anything I could want? But I also am so satisfied and happy with life right now! I love being a wife and an aunt to Lily. I think that is important to always be satisfied and to enjoy every unique season in life. I know that when the time comes it will be amazing... Worth the wait! ♡♡♡ 2005

WORTH THE WAIT (on opposite page) by Elsie Flannigan
SUPPLIES Textured cardstock: Bazzill Basics Paper; Patterned paper: Scenic Route Paper Co.; Acrylic paint: Making Memories; Pen: Sakura; Other: Buttons and thread.

PRECIOUS TO ME by Elsie Flannigan
SUPPLIES Textured cardstock: Bazzill Basics Paper; Stickers: KI Memories and Scrapworks; Other: Buttons and silk flower.

WISDOM by Elsie Flannigan
SUPPLIES Textured cardstock: Bazzill Basics Paper and Prism Papers; Letter stickers: Die Cuts With a View; Stickers: KI Memories and Making Memories; Adhesive jewels: Making Memories; Flower: Prima; Other: Fabric paint and thread.

Make Your Own: Embellished Ribbons

Seriously, who can resist ribbons? They're so pretty and versatile, and there are hundreds of different kinds to choose from, making them a versatile accent for any layout. Plus, it's really fun to design your own ribbon. And you can get so many creative looks. Here's how to create your own embellished ribbon.

LIFE WITH YOU by Mellette Berezoski

SUPPLIES Patterned papers: KI Memories and Anna Griffin; Foam stamps, acrylic paint, dyes, flower brads and decorative brad: Making Memories; Photo anchor: 7gypsies; Other: Bias tape, snap tape and colored rhinestones.

Embellished ribbon samples at right by Elsie Flannigan

step-by-step

Make Your Own: Embellished Ribbons

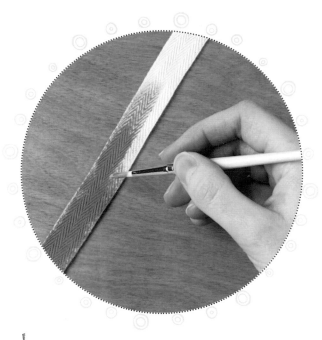

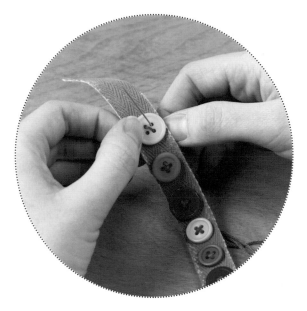

1. Paint white ribbon, twill tape or rickrack with acrylic paint.

2. Add fun embellishments, such as stitching, buttons, flowers, jewels or polka dots.

My Top-10 Style Questions

Scrapbookers often ask me, "How do I discover my true style?" There are so many different approaches you can take—like taking the fun quizzes and challenges in this book, deciding what you think is beautiful and using it on your pages, and looking at other people's work for inspiration.

But sometimes, I like to just sit and think about some questions. And the answers really help guide me. Here, I've listed the top 10 questions I like to ponder. Think about your answers—and maybe they'll inspire you to make a scrapbook page, too!

1   What was your favorite color as a child? What is your favorite color today?

2   What color do you get the most compliments wearing?

3   Who is your style "role model"? Why do you like his or her style?

4   Who is your very favorite author? How does this person inspire you?

5   When you surf the Internet, what websites are your favorites? Why?

6   What's your favorite photo you've taken? What do you love about it?

7   If you could try anything and not fail, what would it be?

8   What is scrapbooking all about to you, anyway?

9   What do you want other people to know about you?

10   Name three words that describe the person you are today. Can you translate those words to your scrapbooking style?

contributor answers

I'm so pleased for the opportunity I had to work with a really exceptional team of designers for this book project. I know you'll find their work just as inspiring and beautiful as I do. I asked each of them to answer the question, "As a scrapbooker, how do you challenge yourself to be creative?" Here are their answers—and one last challenge for you: What would your answer be?

Maria Grace Abuzman

"What do you see? What's right in front of you? What does it mean? For me, nothing inspires me more than attempting to find the truth in the world around me. And the answer is more than I'll ever be able to capture in a page. So I challenge myself each time to re-create just a little of the truth I experience everyday. And by doing so, I see my world in a totally different way."

Mellette Berezoski

"I'm always trying to find different and unique uses for supplies. So many scrapbooking materials can also be incorporated into home decor, party favors, gifts, etc. I love finding new uses for old things. I'm constantly flipping through magazines and catalogs, and rummaging through thrift shops and home improvement stores to get ideas and inspiration. I think it's the most important step in the creative process."

Joy Bohon

"I continually challenge myself—in design, in product use, in my photography. Sometimes I challenge myself to use a product that doesn't automatically seem to fit my style, other times to use different design principles. I'm constantly challenging myself to keep it interesting, to keep it real and meaningful rather than just going with what's 'in' at the time."

Danielle Donaldson

"I find inspiration in illustrations in both art and advertising. I am always challenging myself to create something I love. While my background is in graphic design, my true passion is drawing and painting! Right now, it's all about leaving a little piece of myself in my scrapbook pages.

Vicki Harvey

"I try to find inspiration everywhere. My favorite sources are magazines, catalogs, billboards and my children's clothing. I'll find a design I like and then re-create it with items that can go into my scrapbooks. I like to think outside the box and try and come up with unexpected materials and color combinations."

Rachel Ludwig

"I like to challenge myself by trying to think outside the box. I force myself to try something new or different, or to think creatively. I've done this by using a sketch as a starting point, trying a new concept, etc."

Kendra McCracken

"I find the best time to challenge myself creatively is when I'm feeling stagnant. I'm more willing to risk making a 'mistake.' I find innovative inspiration in graphic design books. I also use my stash of layouts (with styles that are different from my own) and techniques I've clipped from magazines."

Julie Scattaregia

"A great way to creatively challenge myself is to teach each month at my local scrapbook store. Scrappers want to create what they see in the magazines, so it forces me (in a good way!) to keep up with what's hot in the industry. I love to introduce new techniques and show how to use products in fun, unexpected ways."

Danielle Thompson

"I challenge myself by trying to 'forget' what I know about scrapbooking—all of the 'rules' that exist—and just be free with my work. I try to think organically when I'm working on a page; I go with my instincts, no looking back. Sometimes it doesn't work, but when it does, it's very fulfilling."

Traci Turchin

"I love to keep things fresh by switching between layout sizes. It's a great creative boost to work on different sizes of layouts and to incorporate digital elements into my projects!"

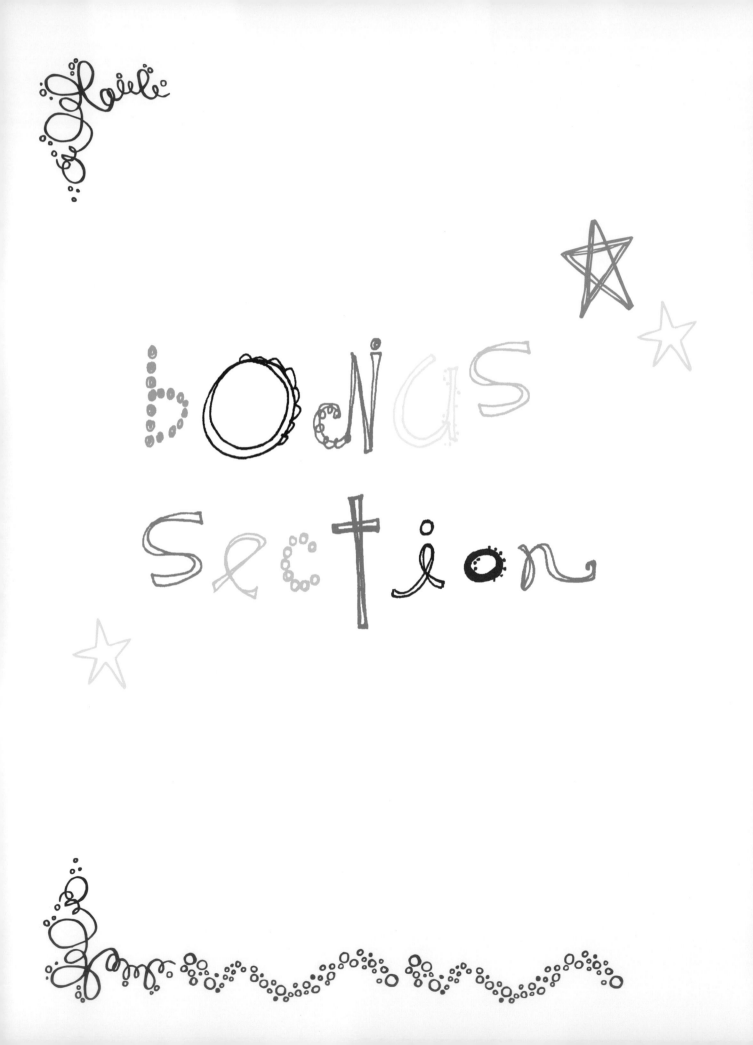

bONuS section

Create Your Own Challenge

I love looking at scrapbook pages. To me, there's nothing more inspirational than seeing a finished page that tells a story with photographs and words and embellishments. I think that's what scrapbooking is really all about, don't you?

I loved seeing the results of the challenges in this book, and thought it would be fun to give you the chance to create your own challenges, too. I've included worksheets and some little hints so you can take these layouts and turn them into your own challenges for yourself and your friends.

How to Create Your Own Challenge

Here's the method I use to create my own challenges: I look at a layout and then go through my little checklist and think, hmmm, what can I try from this page? How does this page inspire me, and what can I do to scraplift it? It's that simple!

To help you create your own challenges, I've included some easy worksheets you can fill in (and photocopy). You don't have to fill in every category. Have fun with these—and let me know what challenges you come up with from the layouts in this book (you never know, maybe I'll take one of your challenges!).

And remember, you can also use these worksheets when you're reading through your favorite scrapbooking magazines. As you complete the worksheets, you'll start to develop a sense of what you love and how you really can find inspiration in almost every layout you see.

elsie's challenge checklist

☐ **Layout Info**
This layout is called ...
This layout was created by ...
I discovered this layout in ...

☐ **Design**
What I think is super cool about the design
of this page is ...
I want to copy this design by ...

☐ **First Impressions**
When I look at this page, I love it because ...
This page inspires me to ...

☐ **Emotion**
This page makes me feel ...
I want to create a page that makes my reader feel ...

☐ **Color**
I can't resist trying the color palette on this
page because ...
I want to try using color to ...

☐ **Technique**
I can't wait to try using this cool technique ...
I never thought about using a product in this way
before ...

☐ **Photography**
The photo on this page makes me feel ...
I want to take a photo like that because ...

☐ **Topics**
I've always wanted to create a page about ...
This layout inspires me to scrapbook about ...

☐ **Embellishments**
The embellishments on this page are ...
I can't wait to experiment with these
embellishments because ...

☐ **Second Impressions**
When I take a second look at this layout, I can't
help but notice ...
This layout tells a story by ...

☐ **Journaling**
The journaling on this page makes me feel ...
I can't wait to try this kind of journaling on
my page because ...

[Hint]

Write your journaling based on the theme of "waiting."

Tick Tock. time is a funny, funny thing. Sometimes it feels like life is flying by and i am seriously shocked at where i am. Other times, not so much. Sometimes i feel like i have been waiting forever and time is moving so slowly. When we got married we thought we would have a baby in the first two years...Now it has been almost 4. It is still a huge desire of ours but i am thankful for the lessons i have learned. Tick Tock for. Our sweet marriage! Enjoying every second!
elsie oct 2005

WAITING by Elsie Flannigan

SUPPLIES Textured cardstock: Bazzill Basics Paper; Patterned paper: Scenic Route Paper Co.; Acrylic paint: Making Memories; Pen: Sakura; Other: Buttons and thread.

[Hint]

Cut elements from patterned paper—like I did with these circles—and use them as embellishments on your page.

PUG IN THE HOOD by Elsie Flannigan

SUPPLIES *Textured cardstock:* Bazzill Basics Paper; *Patterned papers:* KI Memories, American Crafts, Scenic Route Paper Co. and Sassafras Lass; *Paper glaze:* Aleene's Paper Glaze, Duncan Enterprises; *Other:* Buttons and thread.

[Hint]

Look at your photograph for an embellishment you can replicate on your page (like the beautiful flowers here).

GYMBOREE by Joy Bohon

SUPPLIES Patterned papers and tacks: Chatterbox; Rub-ons, epoxy letters and settings: Li'l Davis Designs; Acetate letter: Heidi Swapp for Advantus; Other: Flower punch.

Choose a theme (like "star") and repeat it as many times on your
page as you can.

ROCKSTAR by Elsie Flannigan

SUPPLIES Patterned papers: KI Memories and American Crafts; Ribbon: C.M. Offray & Son; Photo corners: Canson; Tab: 7gypsies;
Rub-ons: Making Memories and KI Memories; Pen: Slick Writer, American Crafts; Other: Staples.

Create a page border with a couple of different strips of sheer eyelet lace.

MY SAVING GRACE by Maria Grace Abuzman

SUPPLIES Patterned papers: Fontwerks and Mari-Mi; Letter stickers and acrylic paint: Making Memories; Rub-ons: Li'l Davis Designs; Chipboard: Heidi Swapp for Advantus; Other: Fabric ribbon.

[Hint]

Enlarge an old black-and-white photograph (even a fuzzy one!) and give it the attention it deserves by framing it with a ton of embellishments.

1953 by Elsie Flannigan

SUPPLIES Textured cardstock: Bazzill Basics Paper; Patterned papers: Scenic Route Paper Co. and Chatterbox; Rubber stamps: Fontwerks; Stamping ink: ColorBox, Clearsnap; Fabric: Amy Butler; Brads: American Crafts and Making Memories; Foam stamps: Li'l Davis Designs; Acrylic paint: Making Memories.

[Hint]

Answer the question "Who is the most soothing person you know?"
on a scrapbook page.

SOOTHING by Elsie Flannigan
SUPPLIES Patterned papers: Wild Asparagus, My Mind's Eye; Chatterbox; Rub-ons: Autumn Leaves; Pen: Uni-ball, Sanford; Acrylic
paint and brads: Making Memories; Transparencies: MOD, Autumn Leaves; Other: Silk flower piece.

[Hint]

Layer an assortment of textures under open chipboard letters.

GIRL by Joy Bohon

SUPPLIES Patterned paper: BasicGrey; Transparency: Art Warehouse, Creative Imaginations; Chipboard stencils, chipboard letters, metal star, metal letter and acrylic paint: Making Memories; Eyelets: Making Memories and Impress Rubber Stamps; Chipboard strip: Heidi Swapp for Advantus.

[Hint]

Create a title with just one letter!

SATISFIED by Elsie Flannigan

SUPPLIES Patterned papers: Autumn Leaves and Chatterbox; Decorative tape, photo corners and acetate star: Heidi Swapp for Advantus; Rub-ons: Making Memories; Pen: Sakura; Other: Staples.

Sew an assortment of patterns together to create a soft, feminine
feel on your page.

DANCE by Vicki Harvey

SUPPLIES Patterned papers: Melissa Frances, Marcella by Kay, Daisy D's Paper Co. and Making Memories; Letter stickers: Mustard
Moon; Gingham ribbon: C.M. Offray & Son; Floral ribbon and lace: Europa Imports; Floral and green decorative tape: Heidi Swapp for
Advantus; Photo corners: Canson; Watch face: Li'l Davis Designs; Pen: Pigment Pro, American Crafts; Flower stamp: Impress Rubber
Stamps; Fabric paint: SoSoft, DecoArt; Decorative-edge scissors: Fiskars; Embroidery floss: DMC; Other: Muslin fabric and vintage buttons.

Find a rare quality of one of your best friends and journal about it.

the <Rare> creative man

Creativity is a continual surprise. —Ray Bradbury

i feel So Lucky tO have A husBand Who is A CReative Soul. Who Loves ARt, music, film And unique food. And Who is Just As PRouD Of our family Scrapbooks as i am. WHat a Blessing!

RARE by Elsie Flannigan

SUPPLIES Patterned papers: BasicGrey and KI Memories; Rub-ons: KI Memories and Fontwerks; Quote sticker: KI Memories; Rubber stamps: Fontwerks; Acrylic paint: Making Memories; Pen: Uni-ball, Sanford; Stamping ink: StazOn, Tsukineko.

[Hint]

Use fabric paint to write your title on a transparency. Allow the paint to dry, then attach your title over a photo.

RED VELVET FASHION by Elsie Flannigan
SUPPLIES Textured cardstock, patterned papers, ribbon and rub-ons: KI Memories; Other: Fabric paint and sequins.

[Hint]

Add a border of sequins to your page.

SIX FLAGS by Elsie Flannigan

SUPPLIES Textured cardstock: Bazzill Basics Paper; Patterned papers, letters and tags: KI Memories; Ribbon: Doodlebug Design and C.M. Offray & Son; Brads: American Crafts and Making Memories; Other: Sequins and staples.

[Hint]

Use conversations with friends and family members as journaling on your pages.

Your response to my black and white photos?

Mom how come you never put the flash on me? I want to be colored.

Here you go baby girl. Is this color enough for you?

FLASH TALK by Joy Bohon

SUPPLIES Textured cardstock: KI Memories; Patterned papers: 7gypsies and MOD, Autumn Leaves; Chipboard letters and acrylic paint: Making Memories; Epoxy letters, rub-ons and pillow buttons: MOD, Autumn Leaves; Pen: Zig Writer, EK Success; Stamping ink: All Night Media; Computer font: Tahoma, downloaded from the Internet.

Increase photo saturation with a photo-editing program.

RETRO STYLE by Elsie Flannigan
SUPPLIES Textured cardstock: Bazzill Basics Paper; Patterned papers: Making Memories and American Crafts; Brads: American Crafts; Acrylic paint: Making Memories; Other: Buttons.

Scrapbook a page horizontally instead of vertically.

MY SAFE PLACE by Elsie Flannigan

SUPPLIES Textured cardstock: Provo Craft and Bazzill Basics Paper; Patterned papers: Scrapworks; Metal flowers: Making Memories; Brads: American Crafts; Rub-on flowers: KI Memories; Ribbon: C.M. Offray & Son; Other: Buttons, rhinestones and fabric paint.

[Hint]

Color coffee filters with watercolors and cut them into shapes to make your own custom page accents.

THE WAY SHE MOVES by Danielle Donaldson

SUPPLIES Brads: Making Memories; Flowers: Prima and Doodlebug Design; Stamping ink and watercolor crayons: Stampin' Up!; Craft ink: Making Memories; Watercolors: Winsor & Newton; Gel medium: Golden Artist Colors; Ribbon: Danielle's own design; Pens: EK Success, Stampin' Up! and American Crafts.

[Hint]

Create a cool title by layering letter stickers inside circle embellishments.

BURNING RUBBER by Kendra McCracken

SUPPLIES Patterned papers: Lasting Impressions for Paper and Junkitz; Mesh: Magic Mesh; Loose-leaf rings: Junkitz; Ribbon: C.M. Offray & Son; Rub-ons: Heidi Swapp for Advantus, Scrapworks and Making Memories; Photo corners and chipboard letters: Heidi Swapp for Advantus; Brads: American Crafts; Foam stamp: Duncan Enterprises; Embossing ink: Stamp-n-Stuff, Stampendous!; Embossing powder: Suze Weinberg, Ranger Industries; Stamping ink: Tsukineko; Embroidery floss: DMC; Other: Acrylic paint and star punch.

[Hint]

Layer, layer and then layer some more!

ME AND MARIE by Elsie Flannigan

SUPPLIES Textured cardstock: Bazzill Basics Paper; Patterned papers: Making Memories and Sassafras Lass; Decorative tape, chipboard letters, photo corners, flower and jewels: Heidi Swapp for Advantus; Stickers: 7gypsies; Acrylic paint: Making Memories; Fabric: Amy Butler; Other: Buttons and thread.

[Hint]

Add hidden journaling beneath a little photo door on your page.

A WINDOW TO MY MIND by Elsie Flannigan

SUPPLIES *Patterned papers: Chatterbox and KI Memories; Quote sticker: KI Memories; Decorative tape: Heidi Swapp for Advantus; Flowers: Prima; Brad and mesh: Making Memories.*

One seed
can start a garden,
one smile
can lift a spirit,
one candle
can light a room...

Look to a greeting card for scrapbook-page inspiration!

GROW MORE BEAUTIFUL by Kendra McCracken

SUPPLIES Textured cardstock: Bazzill Basics Paper; Patterned papers: BasicGrey and Bo-Bunny Press; Mesh: Magic Mesh; Brads, copper buttons and frames, wire pins, metal snaps and epoxy stickers: Tim Holtz for Junkitz; Ribbon: C.M. Offray & Son and May Arts; Chipboard letters and strips: Heidi Swapp for Advantus; Acrylic heart frame: Heidi Grace Designs; Rubber stamps: PSX Design; Flower punch: Marvy Uchida; Stamping ink: Brilliance, Tsukineko; Archival Inks, Ranger Industries; Stampabilities; Fabric paint: Scribbles; Embroidery floss: DMC; Computer fonts: 2Peas Flower Dingbats, downloaded from www.twopeasinabucket.com; Dear Theo, downloaded from www.dafont.com; Other: Rickrack and fabric.

[Hint]

Hand-paint your own floral designs on patterned paper. When they're dry, cut them out and use them as page embellishments.

GRANDBABY by Elsie Flannigan
SUPPLIES Textured cardstock and acrylic paint: Making Memories; Patterned papers: Scenic Route Paper Co.; Decorative tape: Die Cuts With a View; Other: Sequins.

Cut photographs into horizontal strips for a cool graphic look.

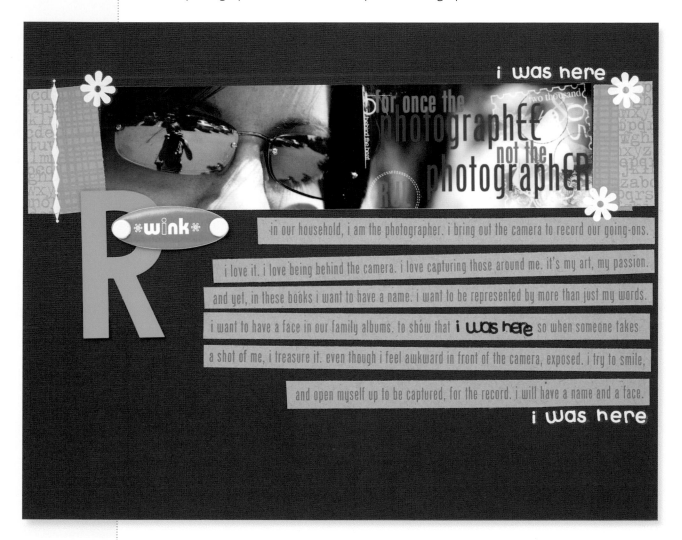

i was here

for once the
photographee
not the
photographer

R *wink*

in our household, i am the photographer. i bring out the camera to record our going-ons.

i love it. i love being behind the camera. i love capturing those around me. it's my art, my passion.

and yet, in these books i want to have a name. i want to be represented by more than just my words.

i want to have a face in our family albums. to show that i was here so when someone takes

a shot of me, i treasure it. even though i feel awkward in front of the camera, exposed. i try to smile,

and open myself up to be captured, for the record. i will have a name and a face.

i was here

I WAS HERE by Rachel Ludwig

SUPPLIES Textured cardstock: Bazzill Basics Paper; Patterned papers: KI Memories; Rub-ons: KI Memories and Fontwerks; Metal letter: American Crafts; Pillow tag: MOD, Autumn Leaves; Brads: American Crafts; Digital brushes: www.8nero.net and Rhonna Farrer, www.twopeasinabucket.com; Computer font: CGPhenixAmerican, downloaded from the Internet.

Add water-colored accents to your pages.

TIGER BY THE TAIL by Danielle Donaldson

SUPPLIES Patterned papers: Danielle's own designs; Brads: Making Memories; Flowers: Prima; Pens: EK Success, Stampin' Up! and American Crafts; Watercolors: Winsor & Newton; Die-cut letters: QuicKutz; Ribbon: Doodlebug Design and Scrapworks.

For a cozy look, stitch around your layout with embroidery floss.

CORNERSTONE by Elsie Flannigan

SUPPLIES Textured cardstock: Bazzill Basics Paper; Brads: American Crafts; Epoxy letters and numbers: Karen Foster Design; Other: Buttons and embroidery floss.

[Hint]

Chronicle your high school fashions on a scrapbook page!

TIMELESS by Elsie Flannigan

SUPPLIES Textured cardstock: Bazzill Basics Paper; Patterned papers: KI Memories, Scenic Route Paper Co. and Die Cuts With a View; Quote sticker: KI Memories; Rub-ons: Scenic Route Paper Co.; Acrylic paint: Making Memories; Flower: Prima; Adhesive jewels: Making Memories; Other: Button and thread.

Journal your beliefs!

FAITH by Maria Grace Abuzman

SUPPLIES Textured cardstock: Bazzill Basics Paper; Patterned paper: foof-a-La, Autumn Leaves; Rub-ons; Fontwerks; Rubber stamps: Fontwerks and Heidi Swapp for Advantus; Stamping ink: Ranger Industries; Bookbinding tape and sticker: Making Memories; Pen: Pigma Micron, Sakura.

Use your favorite song lyrics as a page title.

UNDERNEATH IT ALL by Elsie Flannigan

SUPPLIES Textured cardstock: Bazzill Basics Paper; Patterned paper: Chatterbox; Ribbon: C.M. Offray & Son; Mask: Heidi Swapp for Advantus; Foam stamps: Provo Craft; Pens: Uni-ball, Sanford; Zig Writer, EK Success; Other: Rhinestones.

[Hint]

Journal on tags and "hang" them on your layout.

THIS IS ME by Julie Scattaregia

SUPPLIES Patterned papers: Daisy D's Paper Co.; Metal word, clay letters and bubble word: Li'l Davis Designs; Metal screen, metal frame and metal ampersand: Making Memories; Rub-ons: Daisy D's Paper Co.; Negative strip: Narratives, Creative Imaginations; Stamping ink: Iridescent Ink, Dr. Ph. Martin's; Acrylic paint: Delta Technical Coatings; Ribbon: C.M. Offray & Son; Other: Silk flower and chenille fabric.

Feel free to tell your story in your own way!

PHOTO POET by Danielle Donaldson

SUPPLIES Textured cardstock: Bo-Bunny Press; Patterned papers: BasicGrey; Stamping ink: Ranger Industries; Rub-ons: Making Memories; Letter stickers: American Crafts; Pens: EK Success, Stampin' Up! and American Crafts; Flower: Prima; Other: Ribbon.

[Hint]

Hand-cut brackets from patterned paper to highlight your journaling.

Don't give up on your dreams.

Dreams are soul food.

They keep us alive on the inside.

They burn deep within us, driving us forward to the next stop on our journey of life.

I adore Rhonna! She has an endless supply of energy, creativity [and] passion for her [art]! She totally inspires me to keep [dreaming], keep [growing] and to enjoy the [journey]! Elsie 2005

RHONNA by Elsie Flannigan
SUPPLIES Textured cardstock, patterned papers and stickers: KI Memories; Pen: Sakura; Stamping ink: ColorBox, Clearsnap.

Create a masculine feel on a page by mixing and matching textures.

JUST BECAUSE by Kendra McCracken

SUPPLIES Patterned papers: Karen Foster Design, BasicGrey and 7gypsies; Photo corners and acetate letters: Heidi Swapp for Advantus; Canvas tag: Art Warehouse, Creative Imaginations; Rub-ons and brads: Making Memories; Acrylic letters and conchos: Paper Studio; Ribbon: C.M. Offray & Son; Rubber stamps: PSX Design; Stamping ink: Brilliance, Tsukineko; ColorBox and Fluid Chalk, Clearsnap; Archival Ink, Ranger Industries; Computer fonts: 4990810 and Kingthings Printkit, downloaded from www.dafont.com; Other: Twine, textured cardstock, acrylic paint, fabric, rickrack, photo hanger and jump ring.

Scrapbook the memory even if the photo isn't perfect!

AN AMERICAN GIRL by Julie Scattaregia

SUPPLIES Textured cardstock: Bazzill Basics Paper; Patterned paper, foam stamps, rub-ons, metal frame, bubble letter and number, paper clip, safety pin and embellished backgrounds: Li'l Davis Designs; Label tape: Dymo; Rubber stamps: Postmodern Design; Tag: 7gypsies; Metal photo corner: Embellish It!.

ARTIST by Elsie Flannigan

SUPPLIES Textured cardstock: Bazzill Basics Paper; Patterned papers: KI Memories, BasicGrey and Making Memories; Stickers: KI Memories; Rubber stamps: Fontwerks; Stamping ink: StazOn, Tsukineko; Plastic ring: Junkitz; Acrylic paint: Making Memories.